WOMEN WHO DARED SERIES

GETTING THE REAL STORY

NELLIE BLY AND IDA B. WELLS

SUE DAVIDSON

THE SEAL PRESS

Design by Clare Conrad.

Library of Congress Cataloging-in-Publication Data
Davidson, Sue, 1925-
Getting the real story : Nellie Bly and Ida B. Wells / by Sue Davidson.
    p. cm.
Summary: Parallel biographies of two women who used their journalistic skills to fight against unjust treatment based on sex and race in late nineteenth- and early twentieth-century America.
    ISBN 1-878067-16-8
    1. Readers—Biography. 2. Readers for new literates. 3. Bly, Nellie, 1867-1922. 4. Wells-Barnett, Ida B., 1862-1931. 5. Women journalists—United States—Biography. [1. Bly, Nellie, 1867-1922. 2. Wells-Barnett, Ida B., 1862-1931. 3. Journalists. 4. Afro-Americans—Biography. 5. Women—Biography.] I. Title.
PE 1127.B53D38   1992
070'. 92273—dc20
[B]
                                                        91-38041
                                                        CIP
                                                        AC

Printed in the United States of America.
First printing, February 1992
10 9 8 7 6 5 4 3 2 1
Foreign Distribution:
In Canada: Raincoast Book Distribution, Vancouver, B.C.
In Great Britain and Europe: Airlift Book Company, London

Photo Permissions:
Nellie Bly: cover and xii, courtesy of the Library of Congress; xiv, courtesy of the Pittsburgh Post-Gazette; xiii (map), courtesy of the New York Historical Society; xiii (photo), courtesy of the Library of Congress. Ida B. Wells: cover, 78, 79 and 80, courtesy of the Department of Special Collections, The University of Chicago Library.

Author's Acknowledgments

Although the basic arrangement of this book has not changed since its first draft, a number of generous people helped me bring the text to its final form.

I am much indebted to the valuable critical comments of those who read the manuscript in draft. My special thanks to Seattle reading experts Sandra McNeill, director of Goodwill Literacy Adult Reading Center, who patiently followed several drafts; Becky Allen, literacy coordinator of the Seattle Public Library; Madalene Lickey, Mercer Middle School librarian; Deejah Sherman-Peterson, Washington Middle School librarian; Carletta Wilson, Rainier Beach branch librarian; and also to Lora Myers, writer and literacy curriculum specialist, New York, for her painstaking and perceptive reading. I am deeply grateful for the comment and support of Dorothy Sterling, author of many fine biographies, including the sole biography of Ida B. Wells up to now. Within my own family, I was fortunate to have expert advice on political history from my husband, Alex Gottfried, emeritis professor of political science, University of Washington; and on social and cultural history from my daughter, Erika D. Gottfried, nonprint curator of the Taimiment Institute Library/ Robert F. Wagner Labor Archives, New York University. My loving appreciation to both.

A test edition of chapters from the orginal draft of the book was submitted to Seattle students for their written evaluation of its readability and interest. My warm thanks to Susan Oas, head of the language arts department of Ingraham High School; to Anne

Helmholz, director of the Literacy Action Center; to Ruth Bartrom, language arts department, Marshall Alternative High School; and, again, to Sandra McNeill, for their organizing of the testing and the return of student response forms. My gratitude is due to all the students, faculty, and staff who took part in this process. I am also indebted to my friend Paige Wheeler for blithely accomplishing, in chart form, what seemed to me the maddening task of making statistical sense of student responses. I also wish to thank my friend Cynthia Hallanger, instructor in English as a Second Language, Eastern Washington University, Spokane, for an early, helpful discussion on the design of the instructor response form.

Jennifer McIntyre, of Washington Literacy, gave me guidance by testing first-draft chapters of the book for reading level. Gail Malmgreen, archivist, Robert F. Wagner Labor Archives, kindly provided me with reproduced archival material on Eugene V. Debs that is the basis of my account of Nellie Bly's meeting with him. Edith Ruby, Ingraham High School librarian, helped me to contact appropriate readers and was generally helpful as a school consultant. Last and not least, my Seal Press editor, Faith Conlon, brought to each successive draft of the book an acuteness and sensitivity that any writer is blessed to find in an editor. It is a pleasure to thank each of these people.

For any errors of fact or the interpretation of facts in the imaginative reconstruction of events in the lives of Nellie Bly and Ida B. Wells, I take sole responsibility.

To Alex: y.k.
and
in memory of Aline Reed

These stories contain scenes and details which are imaginary. The basic facts and main events are a true record of the lives of Nellie Bly and Ida B. Wells.

Contents

Introduction

This book tells the stories of two daring North American women. Their names were Nellie Bly and Ida B. Wells. They were both born around the same time, in the early 1860s. Both of them became well known as newspaper reporters. Before this time, although women sometimes wrote articles for newspapers, only a few had ever worked as reporters. Ida B. Wells and Nellie Bly made a path for other women to follow.

Ida and Nellie were alike in other ways, too. Both risked their lives for the things they believed in. Both of them traveled to distant countries. They traveled in the United States, too, and they met many people. But they never met each other.

Nellie and Ida were both often described as nice-looking. They both liked to dress stylishly. Each of them started out in life without much money. Each had to struggle and work hard.

And yet, for all that Nellie and Ida had in common, their lives were very different. For Nellie Bly was white, and Ida B. Wells was black. That is a fact that shaped their lives, their work, and their stories.

NELLIE BLY

Elizabeth Cochran in her youth. At the age of twenty she became a reporter for the Pittsburgh Dispatch. *She used the name "Nellie Bly" for her writing.*

November 14, 1889. On that date, Nellie Bly set sail on her trip around the world. A map showed New York World readers the route she was to take.

January 1890. Nellie Bly when she returned from her around-the-world trip.

In 1887, Nellie Bly took on a daring project. She pretended to be insane so she could get a firsthand report on Blackwell's Island Asylum. This led to reforms in mental hospitals around the country.

Outline of Life Events

May 5, 1864: Elizabeth Cochrane born in Cochran's Mills, Pennsylvania.

1884-85: Moves to Pittsburgh, Pennsylvania, with mother. Under pen name "Nellie Bly," publishes first article, on divorce, in the *Pittsburgh Dispatch*. Is hired as *Dispatch* reporter. Her firsthand reports on working women, slums, and prisons are praised by reformers, but also cause complaints. Is re-assigned to cover "safe" subjects, such as plays and books.

1886-87: Travels in Mexico with her mother. Writes stories exposing Mexican poverty and political corruption. As a result, is expelled from Mexico after six months. Returns to *Dispatch*.

1887: To New York. Gets job as New York *World*'s first woman reporter by writing undercover story on conditions at Blackwell's Island insane asylum. Her story leads to reforms at Blackwell's Island and other U.S. hospitals.

1887-89: Publishes *Ten Days in a Madhouse* and book on Mexico. Works to try to bring about reforms, especially in areas affecting poor women and children, through stories on sweatshops, dishonest employment agencies, jail conditions. Starts around the world, **November 14, 1889**, determined to beat the 80-day record of Jules Verne's fictional character Phileas Fogg.

1890-93: Completes trip successfully in **1890**, gaining world-wide fame. Writes book about global race. Becomes wealthy through lectures, book sales, syndicated newspaper columns.

1894-1914: Continues crusades on behalf of the poor, workers, the elderly, women, children. Investigates Pullman strike; interviews workers and jailed union leader Eugene V. Debs. Marries millionaire manufacturer Robert L. Seaman, **1895**. Retires until his **1904** death, when she takes over his business. Business success followed by financial disaster. Flees to Austria, **1914**.

1914-22: Stranded in Austria by World War I, until **1919**. Returns to U.S., penniless. Goes to work on the New York *Evening Journal*. Takes up cause of abandoned children. Last big story, against capital punishment, is eyewitness account of execution of convicted murderer Gordon Hamby. Dies of pneumonia, **January 22, 1922**, at the age of fifty-seven.

CHAPTER 1

Elizabeth Becomes Nellie

"Elizabeth, please go to bed. It's nearly midnight."

"Not yet, Mother. I want to finish writing this letter. I've never been so angry in my life!"

"All right then, dear. Do as you please." Mrs. Cochrane smiled at her dark-haired daughter's head bent in the lamplight. She knew that Elizabeth almost always did as she pleased.

Now Mrs. Cochrane glanced around the shabby room and sighed. She and Elizabeth had moved four times since coming to Pittsburgh. Each time they moved, it was to a more run-down place. But Elizabeth said their poverty would not last. Soon she would begin to make money from the stories she wrote. Then their fortunes would rise.

Elizabeth was not writing a story tonight. She was writing a letter to the *Pittsburgh Dispatch*. This newspaper had printed an article titled "What Girls Are Good For." The article said that women should not leave their homes to take jobs. It also made fun of the idea that women should be allowed to vote.

"And why shouldn't women have the right to vote!" Elizabeth said. "Isn't it our country, too? How long are we supposed to wait? It's 1885! And how are we going to eat, if we don't have jobs?"

The article said that women should let their husbands take care of them. But twenty-year-old Elizabeth did not want a husband. And Mrs. Cochrane's husband—Elizabeth's father—was dead. He had left some money, but now it was gone.

Mrs. Cochrane and Elizabeth had recently left the little Pennsylvania town that was their home. They had come to nearby Pittsburgh, where Elizabeth's two older brothers ran a small business. Elizabeth's brothers helped their mother and sister with a small allowance. But Elizabeth didn't plan to take their money for long. She was working hard on her stories and trying to sell them.

Mrs. Cochrane had hoped that Elizabeth could find a job teaching school in Pittsburgh. But Elizabeth told her, "There are *fifty* women for *every* teaching job, Mother. There are a hundred women for every decently paid job I've tried to get! Anyway, teaching's not for me. I am a *writer*, Mother."

It was true that Elizabeth wrote well. In fact, when the editor of the *Pittsburgh Dispatch* read her letter, he was impressed. The letter was bold and clear. It pointed out that a very large number of women needed to work for a living. It said that women's brains were just as good as men's. Therefore, the letter asked, why were women kept out of good jobs? Why were they not allowed the right to vote? Why not give women an equal chance, the letter asked, to show what they could do?

Elizabeth had signed her letter "E.C." The *Dispatch* editor, George Madden, wanted to know more about "E.C." "He may have some new ideas for newspaper stories," Mr. Madden thought. Mr. Madden felt sure that "E.C." was a man pretending to be a woman. "No woman could write such a strong letter," he thought.

Elizabeth had not put her address on the letter. So Mr. Madden placed an ad in the *Dispatch*. It said:

"To the gentleman who wrote the letter on women's rights signed 'E.C.': Please send two samples of your writing to the *Dispatch*. Address to Mr. George Madden, editor."

Elizabeth looked through the *Dispatch* ads the next day. She was looking for a cheaper place to live. She and her mother were running very low on money again.

Elizabeth's eye traveled down the page. When she saw Mr. Madden's ad, her heart began to beat fast. She threw down the paper. Then she picked it up, hugged it to her, and waltzed around the room.

Mrs. Cochrane was amazed. She hadn't seen Elizabeth dance—or even smile—for a long time. Elizabeth had too many worries for a girl her age, Mrs. Cochrane thought. But what could Mrs. Cochrane do? The money Mrs. Cochrane sometimes earned at sewing didn't provide a living. There were few ways that a middle-aged woman could earn even half a living.

"Mother, quick! Help me get dressed, please." Elizabeth was scrambling to get into her long petticoats, her high-buttoned shoes. She was laughing. "Gentleman!" she burst out. She flew to her battered desk, snatched up a notebook that lay there.

"Get ready for a shock, Mr. Madden," she thought. "Your 'gentleman' is on her way!"

George Madden rubbed his moustache with his forefinger. "Umm," he said. He finished reading the final page of Elizabeth's notebook. Then he looked at Elizabeth herself, seated on the other side of his desk. He was still surprised to find that 'E.C.' was a woman. "Just a girl, really," he thought. "Doesn't look more than eighteen or nineteen."

Elizabeth's gray eyes gazed cooly back at him. But her knees were trembling. "He's going to say my articles are no good!" she thought. "Oh, why am I making a fool of myself? Why did I force my way in here?"

She had not been content to mail her stories to the *Dispatch* editor. She wanted to make *sure* that he read them. The office boy had tried to keep her out of Mr. Madden's office. But she had said, in a firm voice, "Mr. Madden is expecting me. Tell him that E.C. is here." Behind her, the reporters had whispered and laughed. They were all men. Women did not work in newspaper offices, and were seldom seen there.

Mr. Madden took his forefinger away from his moustache. He tapped the finger on Elizabeth's notebook.

"You sure you wrote these pieces, young lady?"

Now Elizabeth forgot to be afraid that he might think her stories were no good. "Of course I wrote them!" she said. "Why do you think I didn't?"

"Because these articles are about divorce, in lots of detail. How do you know so much about divorce? You don't look old enough to be married, much less divorced."

Elizabeth began to feel more at ease. "My father was a lawyer and a judge," she said. "I used to hear him talk about his divorce cases. I've read his law books, too. Besides," she added, "I have met women who are divorced." This was true. Women who were widows or divorced often had very little money. Like Mrs. Cochrane and Elizabeth, they had to live where rents were cheap. "I've learned a lot from talking with them."

Mr. Madden was thinking hard. In 1885, people were still shocked by divorce. It was a new thing for a woman to write about divorce. "This girl is certainly different," Mr. Madden thought. "She has nerve."

Aloud, he said: "Well, these are interesting stories."

"Then you'll print them?" Elizabeth said.

Mr. Madden made up his mind. "All right," he said. "I'll take all three of them. We'll print them three days in a row. I'll pay you five dollars each."

Five dollars was worth a lot more, in those days, than it is today. To Elizabeth, it sounded like a fortune. But she didn't want to seem too excited. She nodded her head. In a calm voice, she said, "That will be fine."

Mr. Madden got to his feet. He opened the door for Elizabeth. "Another thing," he said. "Do you want to sign your stories with your full name? Or do you want to sign them 'E.C.', or some other name? A lot of our writers use pen names."

Elizabeth thought, "A whole new life is starting for me. I want to begin it with a new name, a pen name. But what name?"

At that moment, the office boy passed by the open door. He was whistling a tune. It was a new popular song called "Nellie Bly." It was one of Elizabeth's favorite songs.

"Nellie Bly," said Elizabeth. "I like that name. From now on, I'll sign my stories Nellie Bly."

Elizabeth's stories on divorce were a success. Pittsburgh newspaper readers were all talking about them. Some did not agree with all the things the stories said. But they wanted to read every word, anyway.

Readers wondered who "Nellie Bly" could be. They argued about it. Some said that Nellie Bly was a man pretending to be a woman. They thought the stories were too bold to be written by a woman. Others said that Nellie Bly *must* be a woman. "She knows more about women than any man could know," they argued.

Because of all this talk, many copies of the *Dispatch* were sold. Mr. Madden was pleased. He asked Elizabeth to write more articles.

Elizabeth's next articles also made readers talk. She wrote about the problems of working women. She went into the factories where they worked. The factories were dirty. They were so dark that the workers could hardly see. The women often hurt themselves at their machines. They worked long hours for low pay. It was not enough money to feed them and their children.

Elizabeth wrote about the slums where the working women lived. The slums were crowded. Many new immigrants lived there, in great poverty. Ten people sometimes shared one small room. There was not enough water for all these people. Nothing could be kept clean. Bugs and rats were everywhere.

Elizabeth's readers were shocked. Many of them had not known how the poor people of Pittsburgh lived. "Something must be done about this," they said. They held public meetings where they talked about the problem. They wrote to public officials, and they went to see them. They demanded clean, decent housing for the low-income people of Pittsburgh.

This was just what Elizabeth had wanted. She wanted to make readers care about the wrongs in society. She wanted to use her writings to make the world a better place.

She wanted other things, too. She wanted to prove that a woman could succeed in "a man's job." She wanted to be a success herself.

Mr. Madden wanted her to succeed, too. He admired her spirit. He admired her for wanting to do some good for people with her writing. So he did an unusual thing. He offered her a job as a reporter for the *Dispatch*.

She didn't have to think twice about accepting.

CHAPTER 2

Fans and Foes

Nellie Bly caused a stir when she first went to work at the *Dispatch*, in the winter of 1885. A woman reporter was something new. The men in the office didn't know what to expect of Nellie.

Like other readers of the *Dispatch*, the newsmen were a little shocked by Nellie. They knew that she had done things that no "lady" would do. "Ladies" did not write about divorce. If a "lady" wrote at all, it was about love, or cooking, or housekeeping. And "ladies" did not go alone into rough neighborhoods, as Nellie had done. In fact, a young "lady" almost never went anywhere alone. "Ladies" were supposed to need someone to protect them on the streets.

Yet Nellie *looked* very ladylike. She wore a prim little hat, with a veil. Her long skirts swept the floor gracefully. She was slender and seemed delicate. Her hands, when she took off her gloves, were soft and smooth.

The newsmen wondered how they should treat Nellie. They wondered if they should stand up when she entered the newsroom. They wondered if they should pull out her desk chair for her. The whole thing made them very nervous.

But Nellie wasn't nervous. She wasn't thinking about how the other reporters ought to treat her. She was thinking about ideas for stories. She was always dashing off somewhere in search of a new story. She didn't have time to think about anything else.

George Madden said to the reporters, "Why don't you stop gawking at Miss Bly? If you worked as hard as she does, you wouldn't have time to gawk."

Yet after a time, Mr. Madden began to worry a little about Nellie. The two of them had become good friends in the months since their first meeting. One day when she was in his office, he said, "It seems to me that you work *too* hard, Nell."

Nellie laughed. "Do I look unhappy?" she asked.

Madden shook his head. In fact, Nellie looked quite happy, healthy, and lively. "No, but I'm afraid that sooner or later you *will* be unhappy. You won't be young forever. You should be having a little fun at your age."

"But I *do* have fun. It's exciting to work as a reporter. It's exciting to be part of the life of a big city like Pittsburgh. I get to meet so many different kinds of people. People at the bottom of the heap. People at the top—"

"Oh," Madden said, "*those* people. That's not what I mean. I mean young people who could be your friends. I mean parties and such. You don't even have a young man!"

Nellie shrugged. "Young men bore me," she said.

"They're so . . . so *young* !"

It was true that young men did not interest Nellie. She wasn't sure why. It may have been that she compared all young men to her father. For Nellie, Judge Cochrane was the ideal man. No young man Nellie had met could measure up to him, in her eyes. That may have been because Judge Cochrane died before Nellie grew up. She had never seen him with the eyes of an adult.

Nellie smiled at George Madden. "Please don't worry about me," she told him. "I had all I wanted of parties and young men, back home. I came to Pittsburgh to be a *writer*. That's all I want now. To write, and to help people with my writing."

"Okay, okay," said Madden. "I give up! You are as stubborn as a post, Nellie." And they went on to talk about other things.

Meanwhile, the *Dispatch* reporters were getting used to being around Nellie. They could see that she wasn't paying much attention to their manners. She didn't seem to expect special treatment, just because she was a woman. So they stopped worrying about how to behave with her.

Some of the reporters became friendly with Nellie. They chatted with her about politics and the city. Sometimes Nellie went with a group of them for lunch or coffee. They talked and argued about newspaper work. For Nellie, this was more fun than going to parties had ever been. She enjoyed "talking shop" with the reporters.

But some of the reporters were not friendly to Nellie. They thought it was wrong for a woman to work as a reporter. They believed that "a woman's place is in the home." Besides that, they were jealous of Nellie's success. They didn't like the attention she got from readers of the *Dispatch*.

And Nellie *did* get a lot of attention. Every day, the mail brought her stacks of fan letters. Women workers wrote to thank her for telling about their harsh working conditions. Reformers thanked her for writing about the evils of the slums. Members of the clergy thanked her for arousing concern about the city's poor. The suffragists—people who wanted women to have the right to vote—were proud of Nellie. They wrote to thank her for showing what women could do.

But some of Nellie's mail wasn't fan mail. Some people were outraged by Nellie's stories. What decent woman would poke her nose into every dirty corner? they asked. These people also wrote to Nellie. They called her, among other things, a "hussy," a "harlot," a "Red." They said she should be run out of town. At the very least, she should be fired from the *Dispatch*.

Some people who wanted Nellie fired didn't bother to write to her. They wrote to Mr. Madden. Or they went to his office to complain to him.

Factory owners complained that Nellie was stirring up trouble among the workers. They said that Nellie was causing workers to join the unions. (Unions were weak at this time, but were getting stronger.) Owners of slum housing also complained. They said that the demands on them were going to put them out of business. Some city leaders also complained to Mr. Madden. They said that Nellie's stories were giving the city of Pittsburgh a bad name.

Mr. Madden had no intention of firing Nellie. He liked her, and he admired her work. All the same, sometimes he worried. The factory owners, landlords, and city leaders were important in Pittsburgh's business world. If the *Dispatch* lost its business friends, it would lose advertisers. And like most newspapers, the *Dispatch* needed the money from advertisements.

But Mr. Madden put off doing anything about his worries. He didn't say anything to Nellie about the complaints.

One day Mr. Madden said to Nellie, "There's a story I want you to do. I met the warden of the new Western Penitentiary at lunch today. He says he has made all sorts of reforms. He says it's a model prison. I'd like you to go out there and talk with him."

Nellie said, "Of course, I'd want to do more than talk with the warden. I'd want to inspect the whole prison. There's no other way to know if he's telling the truth."

"I think he'll let you inspect it. But go—and find out!"

The warden showed Nellie through the prison. The prisoners' cells were clean. The kitchen was clean, and the meals were nourishing. There was a library. There were shops where the men could learn a trade. Nellie interviewed a number of prisoners. They said that they were well-treated.

Nellie wrote an article that praised the new prison. In most prisons, Nellie wrote, the men were starved or given rotten food. They had no exercise, they were taught nothing. They were regularly beaten up. Western Penitentiary had none of these evils. It should be an example for all other prisons, she wrote.

When the story was printed, a public storm broke loose. Readers were more shocked by Nellie than they had ever been before. What kind of woman, people asked, would show herself to all those rough men? What other woman would go into the very cells where the men slept? What woman would spend her time talking with criminals? Only a woman with no shame and no morals! Only Nellie Bly!

Prison wardens and public officials were angry, too. They didn't like Nellie's remarks about the jails and prisons *they* controlled. Nellie wanted prisons to be like fancy hotels, they said. It was just like Nellie Bly to want to "coddle" criminals!

The very word "crime" was enough to get most people angry. Very few were willing to listen to reason on the subject. Nellie had finally been too daring and had gone too far.

Mr. Madden backed down.

He didn't back down all the way. He didn't fire Nellie. Instead, he asked her to do a new job for the *Dispatch*. This was a job that would probably not get her into so much trouble.

"Nell," he said, "I want you to report on plays for a

while. Until the storm blows over. I'd like you to write our book reviews for a few weeks, too."

Nellie said, "You're the boss."

But she was deeply hurt. She had looked up to George Madden almost like a father. She had thought he was a strong, brave man. She could bear the nasty things people said about her. But she had counted on George Madden to back her up.

Nellie dutifully went to the openings of new plays. Her mother went with her. Mrs. Cochrane enjoyed going to plays. She enjoyed seeing Nellie dressed up for the theatre. She was proud of her lovely young daughter. But . . . ."You look so sad, dear," Mrs. Cochrane said. "Aren't you enjoying yourself?"

No, Nellie was not enjoying herself. For Nellie Bly, this kind of work was much too tame.

CHAPTER 3

In Mexico

"Too tame! Too tame!" Nellie thought, as she dressed that morning.

Standing at the mirror, she pinned up her hair. She brushed her curly bangs over her forehead. "Too *tame!*" She put on her dark blue hat, pulled the veil over her eyes. "I might as well be teaching school as doing *this.*" She made a face and stuck out her tongue at the mirror.

A while later, Nellie got off a horse-drawn streetcar. She marched through the *Dispatch* newsroom and entered George Madden's office. "I'm going to Mexico," she said.

Mr. Madden's mouth opened, but at first nothing came out. He fingered his moustache. "You're going where?" he said.

"To Mexico. To get some stories."

"I'm not sending you to Mexico!" Madden said.

"I know. But I'm going," Nellie said.

"But you can't! It's dangerous! There are riots going on. The country's full of bandits. It's no place for a woman to go alone. Why, *men* have gone there from the United States and never come back. Never heard from again!"

"I'm not going alone. Mother is going with me."

"*Mother!*" Mr. Madden almost shouted. "What good is that?"

Nellie pretended not to hear this. "You're certain to hear from *me*—if you want to. You'll want to buy my stories for the *Dispatch*. Won't you?"

Mr. Madden was silent. He knew he couldn't stop Nellie. And firsthand news from Mexico was hard to get.

"I'll pay my own way," Nellie said. "But if I send stories, the *Dispatch* will want to pay some of my expenses."

Mr. Madden began to laugh. "For an idealist, Nellie, you drive a hard bargain! Okay, okay! It's a deal."

So Nellie Bly set out for Mexico. It was the winter of 1886, and she was twenty-one. It was the first time she had ever set foot outside of Pennsylvania.

Shafts of morning sunlight fell across the bed. Somewhere doves were cooing. Somewhere a rooster crowed. Nellie woke.

She put her feet down on the cool tiles of the floor and went to the window. She threw open the wooden shutters. Below her, the patio blazed with color. Flowers—red, pink, purple, orange, white—bloomed in big clay pots.

Nellie and her mother had reached Mexico City the night before. They were now at the house of Señora

Luna, where they had rented rooms. It had been a long journey on the train. On the way, they had stopped overnight in shabby Mexican towns. The beds were bad; they were also kept awake by heat and flies. Mrs. Cochrane was tired by the time they got to Mexico City.

Señora Luna's house was clean and comfortable. Mrs. Cochrane told Nellie: "Don't wake me tomorrow morning. I'm going to rest in this wonderful bed all day!"

"Buenos días, señorita! Buenos días, buenos días!"

This Spanish greeting came from the parrot on Nellie's balcony. Nellie was glad to practice Spanish— even if it was only with a parrot. "Buenos días (Good morning)!" she said to the parrot. "Cómo esta usted (How are you)?"

Nellie poured water from a pitcher into a basin. She talked with the parrot as she washed. Then she dressed quickly and went downstairs.

Nellie found Señora Luna seated in the cool, dark dining room. She was a large woman with a mass of beautiful black hair. At one corner of her mouth was a small mole, which disappeared when she smiled. She smiled now, at Nellie.

"Buenos días," she said. "Did you sleep well, señorita?"

"Perfectly!" Nellie said.

"And Señora Cochrane? She is still very tired?"

"Too tired to go out with me today," Nellie said. "She'll be fine after a day's rest."

Señora Luna rang a small bell. A servant brought in fruit and coffee. "You are going *out*, Señorita Cochrane?" Señora Luna said. "You are going out— without your mother?"

"Mother won't mind that," Nellie said. "She has plenty of time to go sightseeing later on."

"But, señorita, you must not go out alone! You must go with Señora Cochrane or with a gentleman! It is not done for a young lady to be in public alone!"

Nellie smiled at Señora Luna. "Ah, señora," she said gently, "but I am an *American* young lady!" That seemed to settle the matter for Nellie. She calmly ate her grapefruit. Señora Luna watched her, puzzled. But she said no more on the subject.

Nellie knew that being "an American young lady" didn't really settle anything. She knew that in her own country "young ladies" were not "free and equal." "Gentlemen" were free to come and go as they pleased. "Ladies" were not. They were supposed to be too helpless to be on their own.

But Nellie wanted to show that a woman could take care of herself. So she set out once again, in Mexico, to prove it.

On that first day, and many other days, Nellie toured Mexico City by herself. Alone, she went to churches and palaces. She wandered through museums and public gardens, alone.

Everywhere she went, curious eyes watched her. The men, especially, stared at her. Sometimes they made rude remarks to her. One time some men followed her, calling her names.

If Nellie was uneasy, she didn't show it. And she certainly didn't let her readers know it. In her first story for the *Dispatch,* she wrote about Señora Luna's warning. She said that most people agreed with Señora Luna. She told about the stares of people on the streets. Then she wrote: "But I show them that a free American girl can go anywhere without the help of a man."

Of course, Nellie wanted to "show" the people at home, too! But soon there was much more she wanted to show them.

As Nellie walked the city, she saw beggars everywhere. Everywhere, too, she saw the homeless. She saw whole families living on the streets. Their clothes were rags. Their food was any garbage they could scrape together. They were worse off than even the poorest of Pittsburgh.

Meanwhile, the rich lived in big houses, guarded by iron gates. Making herself known as a travel writer, Nellie was invited into some of their homes. They served costly food and wines. They wore beautiful new clothes. Nellie saw the stables where they kept their horses. The horses lived better than the poor people of Mexico.

As always, Nellie was angered by the injustice she saw. She wrote with passion about the contrasts in the lives of rich and poor. Readers of the *Dispatch* were touched by these stories. Everyone was eager to read them. Far away in Mexico, Nellie didn't seem like such a menace. Complaints about her died down.

Mr. Madden wrote Nellie, suggesting that she come home. He said he wanted to give her back her old job as a reporter. But Nellie wasn't ready to go home. She wanted to see more of Mexico.

Mexico's new President had talked a lot about his plans to develop the silver mines. Nellie wanted to see the mines for herself. The mines were far out in the wilderness. There were no railroads out there. So Nellie hired guides to take her by mule.

Mrs. Cochrane said, "Elizabeth, this is dangerous. Everyone knows the wilderness is full of bandits!"

"Yes," Nellie said, "no wonder. The bandits are just more poor people who have been driven to crime."

"That may be," said Mrs. Cochrane. "But it doesn't change the facts. They still hold up strangers for ransom. Especially gringos. They think that all North Americans have money."

But nothing could change Nellie's mind. In the end, she went. And Mrs. Cochrane went with her. "I'd rather face a bandit than stay here and worry about you," she said.

They did not fall into the hands of bandits. But the journey was hard. In some places, there were no roads. The guides made paths, hacking through bushes. There were steep hills to climb, everyone hanging onto the mules. More than one night, Nellie and her mother slept on the ground.

Nellie sat up late by the campfires, writing in her notebook. When they got back to Mexico City, her article about the journey was all but complete.

Nellie didn't know it, but her visit to Mexico, too, was complete. Word had come back to the Mexican government about Nellie's articles. During her six months in Mexico, Nellie had not only written about the misery of the poor. She had also written an angry report on the Mexican government. She had called it corrupt and accused it of robbing the people. Worst of all, she charged, the government did not permit free dom.

> Mexican papers never publish a word against the government or its officials. People dare not breathe a word against them. Editors are thrown into prison for even hinting that the government needs improvement.

Nellie had only written the truth. But, as had happened before, the truth got her into hot water. A letter was waiting for her at Señora Luna's house. It was stamped with a government seal. It told her that she was no longer welcome in Mexico.

"Buenos días!" the parrot called gaily from the balcony.

But Nellie called back: "Adiós (Goodbye)!"

Taking the World by Surprise

When Nellie returned to the *Dispatch*, Mr. Madden doubled her salary. He also let her go back to reporting. Readers of the *Dispatch* were asking for more of Nellie's stories. Most of them had forgotten that they used to think Nellie was dangerous. And anyway, her stories from Mexico had been so interesting! They forgave her.

But Nellie wasn't sure that she forgave *them*. Besides, Pittsburgh seemed dull after Mexico. Nellie felt restless. She began making faces at herself in the mirror again. "Too tame!" she said to the gray-eyed young woman who looked back at her.

"Mother—what's the most exciting newspaper in the country?"

Mrs. Cochrane looked up from her sewing. "Oh, the paper Nellie Bly writes for," she said. "The *Dispatch*, of course!"

"Oh, *Mother*! How can you say that?"

"Why not, Elizabeth? It's just a matter of opinion!"

"*I* say Mr. Pulitzer's paper, the *New York World*! *That's* the most exciting newspaper in the country! Maybe in the world."

"Why not in the *universe*, while you're at it?" said Mrs. Cochrane. She sighed. "I think I can guess what's coming next."

"Yes," Nellie said. "I want to be a reporter for the *World*. Of course . . . it means I'll have to move to New York."

"Don't you think it would be a good idea to write ahead first? To make sure the *World* is ready to give you a job?"

"Oh," said Nellie, "I already did that. The editor turned me down. But after all, it's Mr. Pulitzer who owns the *World*! The editor just works for him. I'll have to get in to see Mr. Pulitzer himself. Take him by surprise, the way I did with Mr. Madden."

Mrs. Cochrane said no more. She didn't argue when Nellie quit her job at the *Dispatch*. In three weeks, Nellie took a train to New York City. Mrs. Cochrane would follow when Nellie got a steady job. Meanwhile, Nellie moved into a tiny room.

There was just space enough for Nellie's clothes and a few keepsakes from Mexico. Sitting beneath a big Mexican hat hung on the wall, Nellie went to work. She wrote articles about Mexico. She went out and sold them to newspapers and magazines. And almost every day, she visited the offices of the *World*.

But she could not get in to see Joseph Pulitzer. The editor said, "Mr. Pulitzer has no time for women writers. We don't publish love stories or recipes."

"I am a *reporter*!" Nellie said. "Just let me show Mr. Pulitzer the stories I wrote for the *Pittsburgh Dispatch*."

"You can leave them with me," said the editor.

But Nellie would not do that. She wanted to make *sure* that Mr. Pulitzer read her articles. She wanted to talk with him face to face, too. She admired him greatly.

A Jewish immigrant from Hungary, Mr. Pulitzer had once been very poor. He had worked his way to the top. He wanted to make his adopted country a better place. The *World* was a crusading newspaper. It uncovered wrongs and held them up to the light of day. "*My* kind of newspaper!" Nellie thought. So she went on making visits to the *World*.

The office boy groaned loudly when he saw her. "It's *her* again!" The reporters chuckled or smiled. "You'd better run home, little girl," one said. Another said kindly, "A newspaper office isn't a place for a nice young lady like you."

Nellie didn't get angry. In fact, she almost laughed. She thought: "An office is probably a better place for you, Mister. I don't think you'd do so well in Mexican bandit country!"

Then something clicked in Nellie's mind. "Nice young lady?" They wouldn't expect a *lady* to rush Mr. Pulitzer's door! "It wouldn't be *nice*," thought Nellie.

She moved to Mr. Pulitzer's door. The office boy was standing near it. He moved to block her path.

"I *told* you, lady. You can't go in there."

Nellie shoved him out of the way. His mouth fell open. He was so surprised, he couldn't move. Nellie turned the handle and walked gracefully inside. She closed the door behind her calmly.

The man behind the big desk was thin and frail. His head was large. He had large eyes—sad, gentle, and alert.

"Mr. Pulitzer," Nellie said, "I'm sorry to disturb you. But I've been trying to see you for a long time." She went up to the desk. She held out her hand. "I'm Nellie Bly, recently of the *Pittsburgh Dispatch*. Perhaps you've heard of me?"

Mr. Pulitzer's thick eyebrows drew together in a frown. He didn't shake her hand. "How did you get in here?" he said.

"I . . . well. I'm afraid I knocked over your office boy!"

Mr. Pulitzer stared at dainty-looking Nellie. Then suddenly, he laughed. He took her hand. "Be seated, Miss Bly."

Nellie got right down to business. "I want to write for the *World*," she said. "I've brought clippings of my stories."

Mr. Pulitzer read rapidly. He nodded his head. "Yes," he said. "Some of these are remarkable. It takes daring to do this, yes. Particularly for a woman! But— even for a man. However—" He spread his hands. "We have many good reporters."

"You don't have one who will get the story *I* will get!" Nellie's tone was dramatic. "I'll write an eyewitness story about the insane asylum on Blackwell's Island! Everybody whispers about the horrors of that place. But there's no proof. I'll get proof!"

Nellie rushed on breathlessly. "I've heard the asylum is run like a prison. Sick people shouldn't be there! They are there only because they're poor. They can't go anywhere except to a public asylum, like Blackwell's. And they can be mistreated there, too, because they're poor. Nobody cares about them."

Joseph Pulitzer was amazed by Nellie's outburst. But he was even more amazed by her idea for a story. Like divorce, in 1887 insanity was a subject people didn't talk about openly. It was thought of as a shameful illness. He said slowly:

"There is much in what you say, Miss Bly. But Blackwell's Island is closely guarded. How do you propose to get inside to gather material for a story?"

"I'll have to pretend to be insane. I'll have to get myself committed to the insane asylum."

Now Mr. Pulitzer was even more amazed. It was a serious thing to be declared insane. Once done, it was not easily undone. Those who entered the dreaded Blackwell's Island asylum seldom returned. Who would take a chance on being trapped there?

Mr. Pulitzer shook his head. "Maybe you could get inside," he said. "Just *maybe*. But how could we get you *out*?"

Nellie smiled. "You said *we*! Does that mean you would try? Does that mean you'd print my story, if I can get it?"

"Of course we would print such a story! How could we *not* print it? What I can't be sure of is that we could get you out! I'll have to talk with our lawyers about it.

I'm not sure it's right to let you risk the horrors of that place, either."

"Poor people have to face those horrors all the time, Mr. Pulitzer," Nellie said, "with nobody even *trying* to help *them*. Isn't that the point? That exposing this story might help them?"

Nellie's legs had begun to tremble. She half hoped that Mr. Pulitzer would say, "No! I won't have anything to do with it." She was beginning to feel frightened. "What am I letting myself in for?" she thought. "Maybe I really *am* crazy. All this, just for the chance of getting a story? Just to work for the *World*?"

Mr. Pulitzer said, "You seem very sure that your insanity will be believed. I do not know how careful the doctors are about admitting patients. But it may not be easy to fool them."

"I'll succeed," Nellie said. "I am a very good actress."

Mr. Pulitzer asked Nellie to return in forty-eight hours. At that time, they could discuss everything with a lawyer.

Nellie said goodbye to Mr. Pulitzer. Her knees shook harder as she rose. Tears blinded her as she swept past the reporters and the office boy. She was *really* scared to death now!

But no one guessed. Her exit was as calm as her entrance.

As she had said—Nellie Bly was a very good actress.

CHAPTER 5

Crashing the Gates of Hell

A new boarder had moved into the house for "gentle-women" on Second Avenue. She had arrived today, with one small bag. Her trim little suit was the same color as her large gray eyes. She spoke with a Spanish accent. She said she was from Cuba. She didn't say much else. Her name was Miss Brown. Nellie Brown.

But her name wasn't Nellie Brown. It was Nellie Bly. She was upstairs in her room, making faces at the mirror. They were not the kind of faces she usually made. Her eyes stared blankly. Her mouth opened in a shriek, even though no sound came out.

Nellie was practicing her "insanity" act. She had been practicing it for two weeks. Tonight, at last, she planned to use it. She planned to "go crazy" in front of the other boarders.

Part of her act was to seem to be very frightened. "That won't be hard," Nellie thought. "I *am* frightened!" True, the *World* lawyer had said he'd be able to get her out of the asylum. But Nellie had told him she wanted to stay there at least a week. She needed that time to find out everything she wanted to know. Meanwhile, she would not be able to get in touch with anyone. No one must know who she really was. If anyone found out she was a reporter, that would be the end.

Right now, she had not even gotten *into* the asylum. It was time to put that part of the plan to work. She went downstairs.

She joined the other boarders at the dinner table. At first, she was very quiet. When the women spoke to her, she mumbled a few shy words. They were a mix of Spanish and English.

Then, suddenly, Nellie pushed away her plate. "Poison!" she cried. She stared wildly at the women. "You want to kill me!"

She ran from the table to a corner of the room. There, she sank to the floor. She covered her eyes with her hands. She was shaking. She began to sob. "No más! Don't kill me!"

The boarders tried to comfort Nellie. So did the landlady. "No one wants to hurt you!" the women said. But Nellie shrank back from them with a scream. She lay sobbing on the floor.

The women thought that Nellie had lost her mind. "Poor thing," she heard the landlady say. "I don't know who she is. There's no address in her bag. I'll have to call the police."

The police brought Nellie before a judge. The judge, too, felt sorry for this gentle-looking young woman. When he sent her to be examined by doctors, he called some news reporters. "Maybe you can help find out who Nellie Brown is," he said. "Write something. Her family or friends may be looking for her."

At Bellevue Hospital, five doctors examined Nellie. They saw her blank stare. They listened to her wild words about plots to kill her. Then they ordered her to be sent to Blackwell's Island.

Now Nellie was too happy to feel afraid. For one thing, she was glad that the papers would carry a story on "Nellie Brown." That way, Mr. Pulitzer would know that she was on Blackwell's Island. (Only Mr. Pulitzer and the *World* lawyer knew the new name Nellie had taken. Nellie thanked her stars that Mrs. Cochrane didn't know!)

But more than that, Nellie was thrilled with her success. Her act had fooled everybody. She was going to get her story!

Nellie's happy feelings didn't last long. They were soon replaced by anger. The boat that took her and six other patients to Blackwell's Island was a rotten tub. Its decks were slimy. Everywhere Nellie looked, there was dirt. There was not one clean place to sit down. But worst of all were the women guards, called matrons.

The matrons were supposed to be "taking care" of the patients. Nellie soon saw what that meant. They pushed and shoved the patients, cursing them. Most of the patients were quiet or mumbling to themselves. But one patient cried and screamed. The matrons tied her to a bench, slapping her hard.

That was only the beginning. To enter Blackwell's Island asylum was like going through the gates of hell.

Nellie saw a gloomy stone building with bars at the windows. A moment later, she was in a large, bare hall, filled with women. They wore only thin, patched dresses, although it was cold. Some babbled. Some tore at their clothes. Some, their eyes empty, walked in endless circles. Nellie's heart raced with fear.

Two nurses were standing near Nellie. They were chatting and laughing. An old, bent woman went up to them. She was shivering. "Could I have a shawl, please?" Nellie heard her say. She had a quiet, polite voice. The nurses did not answer. "If I can't have a wrap, could I go to bed? I think I have a chill," the old woman said. One of the nurses glared at her.

"The rooms are locked during recreation. You'll stay right where you are. And you'll shut up that complaining, too."

"*Recreation*?" Nellie thought. "Is that what *this* is?"

Then Nellie's name was called. With the other new patients, she was checked into the asylum. She became an inmate of Ward 6, for the less violent cases. She learned that "recreation" meant just about nothing. On some days, inmates were led out and marched around a cold courtyard. There were no other programs for the inmates—unless torment counted.

The inmates lived in torment—or neglect—from the time they rose at 5:30 a.m. They had their first meal of the day—if they could swallow it. Much of the food that came from the dirty kitchen was rotten. Often bugs got to it first.

Supper was at 5:30 p.m. Before bed, three nights a

week, the inmates had baths. These nights were a special torment. The bath water was ice cold. The inmates shared the same few dirty towels. (Nellie dried herself with her nightgown.)

With their hair still sopping, the inmates went to bed. They had only one thin blanket for cover. Their nightgowns were thin rags. Every night, even without baths, they were cold.

The days were no better. In the morning, the inmates cleaned their rooms. Some scrubbed floors and did other heavy work. Those who would not do this were punished. They might be hit or locked into their rooms. Women in Nellie's ward might be sent to the locked ward for the most dangerous cases.

The locked ward was guarded by the matrons. They boasted openly about how they kept order there. They beat the inmates with straps and broom handles. Sometimes they tied them up in a closet, or starved them. Everyone was afraid to be sent to the locked ward.

In Ward 6, most of the day was spent sitting or wandering around the dreary "recreation" hall. After a while, Nellie lost her fear of the other inmates. She began to talk with them.

Some of the women were very ill; they made no sense. But others were as sane as Nellie herself. The old woman Nellie had seen the first day, Mrs. Benson, was one of them. Her only relative, a middle-aged nephew, had lived with her in her small house. When he married, his wife wanted Mrs. Benson out of the house. They had managed to have the old woman declared insane.

Another woman, Flo, had a speech defect. Her employer had gotten angry at her and sent for the police. A judge had sent Flo to Bellevue. Flo was able to explain her problem to Nellie. But she had not been able to make the doctors understand.

One young woman, called Anne, had broken down when her lover died. She was still on the edge but trying to get better. Her bodily health was still poor. She was skin and bones. "How can she get well in a place like this?" Nellie thought.

And if Anne did get better, thought Nellie, who would notice? For Nellie herself had stopped pretending to be insane. And it had made no difference!

She did not expect the nurses to notice the change in her. Clearly, they didn't care if inmates were sick or well. They just wanted to be put to as little trouble as possible. But Nellie had thought that the doctors might care. If their patients improved, wasn't it their job to know that? And to help them get still better?

So Nellie talked to the doctors. She had never been away from Cuba before, she told them. She said she'd been frightened by her new surroundings. "It was an attack of nerves," she said, "and it's over. I am quite well. You should be planning to discharge me soon."

The doctors smiled. "You need a lot of care," they said.

"I am not getting very much care here," Nellie said. "And I am perfectly sane. If you don't believe it, test me."

"Oh, yes," said the doctors. "We'll do that. Tomorrow."

But "tomorrow" never came. Each time Nellie saw the doctors, she asked them to test her sanity. They did nothing. They could not tell who was sane and who was not! And they would not even *try*. Nellie saw that without outside help, *no one* could leave Blackwell's Island. Insane or sane—a life sentence!

Nellie began to feel a touch of panic. She wondered where *her* outside help was. A week had passed, or—was it more? "How many days *have* I been here?" she thought. She was beginning to feel weak. She had eaten almost none of the rotten, evil-tasting food. How could her mind work without food? "Am I starving?" she thought.

Day after day she grew more afraid of the nurses. Often, she protested the way they treated the inmates. "You'd better shut up," the nurses said. We'll send you to the locked ward!" Nellie thought: "Will they do it some day? Will I *die* here?"

Then, with an effort, Nellie pulled herself together. "I'm here to get a story," she thought. "If I'm going to help these women, I *must* get out. I *will* get out! Of course I will!"

And she did. Ten days after she entered Blackwell's Island, on October 5, 1887, Nellie left. On the arm of the *World*'s lawyer, she walked through the barred gates. She walked out into the sunlight of her world. Into freedom.

Who's Afraid of Nellie Bly?

Nellie soaked for an hour in a warm tub. It felt wonderful! She dried her long hair, glancing around her room. It was only a tiny room in a shabby boarding house. But, to Nellie, it looked like a heavenly palace.

She thought of the women she had left behind, in the asylum. Her eyes filled with tears. She sat down beneath the Mexican hat that hung on the wall. Pen in hand, she began to write:

"The Insane Asylum on Blackwell's Island is a human rat-trap. It is easy to get in, but once there, it is impossible to get out . . . . "

Nellie wrote page after page, working late into the night. She was still tired from sleepless nights at the asylum. But she wanted to write while her experiences were fresh in her mind.

The next Sunday, the *World* printed the first of Nellie's two asylum stories. It appeared under a huge headline. The headline read: "BEHIND ASYLUM BARS, by Nellie Bly."

By Monday, the paper was sold out. Nellie's eyewitness story became the talk of New York. Before long, it became the talk of the nation, too. Newspapers all over the country wrote about the daring and courage of the "girl reporter."

Once again, Nellie had done something new in her time. Nobody had written about an asylum from the viewpoint of an inmate. Mr. Pulitzer now fully grasped that young Miss Bly was not an ordinary reporter. She was put on the *World* payroll immediately. She was given a desk at the *World*, becoming its first woman reporter.

But there were far wider results from Nellie's asylum stories. As she had hoped, her stories led to changes for the insane poor.

First, the city's Board of Charities sent a team to investigate Blackwell's asylum. The team asked Nellie to go, too. News of the team's visit had leaked out in advance. So, of course, the place had been prettied up. The dirty walls were freshly painted. There were new, warm blankets on some beds. The kitchen was cleaner, and it was stocked with fresh food.

But this did not fool the team. They could see that these improvements had been recently made. There were price tags on some of the new blankets. The patients still looked starved and sickly. Furthermore, it was plain that matrons, nurses, and doctors were telling lies. Their accounts of the asylum's daily routine did not agree.

It was clear that the asylum was not run properly. The main problem was lack of money. Money was needed to pay decent wages, to attract well-trained doctors and nurses. Money was needed to buy food, blankets, clothes, and equipment. The Charities Board had often asked the city for more money for the asylum. But the city had never been willing to give it.

Until now. Three weeks after Nellie's stories appeared, the *World* ran another asylum story. Its headlines read:

THE *WORLD* THEIR SAVIOR
How Nellie Bly's Work Will Help
The City's Insane

The story reported that the city had granted additional money to Blackwell's Island asylum. It was more than a million-and-a-half dollars. Over two million more was granted for the city's other insane asylums. The reforms were already under way.

The changes came too late for old, frail Mrs. Benson. Nellie learned that she had died of pneumonia. She learned about this in a letter from Anne. Anne had recovered her health, and was "outside." Not long after, Flo was also released.

News of insane asylum reform flowed in from many parts of the country. Mr. Pulitzer was proud of Nellie's part in these reforms. He saw to it that she had a privileged place at the *World*. Unlike the other reporters, she did not have to wait to be assigned to a story. She was allowed to use her own ideas for stories. And she had plenty of ideas.

To get her true stories, Nellie often played a part. Dressing and speaking like an immigrant, she investigated New York's employment agencies. The agencies, she found, took their fees in advance. They might send a non-English-speaking immigrant to a job where English was required. Or they might send immigrants to places where there weren't jobs at all. Confused and helpless, most immigrants did not try to get their money back. In any case, the agencies refused to return it.

As she had done in Pittsburgh, Nellie went into the factories where women worked. She wore an old dress, a shawl over her head. She managed to get jobs at a box factory and at a china factory. In both places, she found children—some as young as eight—working alongside women. Like the adults, the children worked twelve and fourteen hours a day. For a few pennies, they labored in dark, dirty rooms, under dangerous conditions.

Uncovering one abuse after another, Nellie reported on them in the *World*. She even reported on jail conditions for women, from the inside. She managed this by paying a woman to accuse her of stealing money from the woman's purse. The woman was a stranger Nellie met in a park. As Nellie had arranged, the woman never showed up in court; and Nellie was freed. Meanwhile, however, she had spent a frightening night in jail.

Some of Nellie's stories led quickly to reforms. This happened, for example, in the city's jails. Nellie had protested against the searching of female prisoners by male guards. After her jail story, women were hired to handle female prisoners. Other jail conditions for women were also improved.

It was to be quite a while, however, before factory conditions improved. And when that did happen, it was largely because of labor unions. Still, Nellie's protests helped. The public was especially moved by her stories about child workers. Her reports helped pave the way for enforcement of laws against child labor.

Meanwhile, people who misused the poor began to fear Nellie. They never knew if some bright eyes might be hers—looking for trouble. Since she went around in disguise, how would anybody know—until they read about their misdeeds in the *World*? "Who's afraid of Nellie Bly?" was a good question in New York during the late 1880s. Some would have answered: "Everybody!"

Well—*nearly* everybody. There were at least two people who weren't afraid of Nellie. One of them was her mother.

When Nellie went to work for the *World*, she sent for her mother. Mrs. Cochrane found an apartment for herself and Nellie. She shopped for the furnishings.

"Buy everything you want, Mother," Nellie said grandly. She was making a good salary now. She was proud of it.

Mrs. Cochrane said, "Maybe not quite *everything*." Mrs. Cochrane had been through good times and bad. She liked to live well. At the same time, she believed in saving for a rainy day.

Mrs. Cochrane was proud of Nellie's success. But,

again, she thought about rainy days. Nellie was twenty-three. It would be a rainy day, Mrs. Cochrane thought, if she woke up at twenty-five, unmarried.

"You should be thinking about settling down, Elizabeth," Mrs. Cochrane said. "You won't be twenty-three forever. It's time to start thinking about marriage."

"Good heavens. I don't *want* to settle down, Mother!"

"By the time you do, it may be too late. Do you think Mr. Metcalf, for instance, is going to wait forever?"

"I don't know. He hasn't asked me to marry him for a week." Nellie laughed. "Maybe he's taking me for granted!"

James Metcalf was a journalist. Mr. Pulitzer had introduced him to Nellie. Nellie and Jim had quickly become friends. They had begun to see each other often.

Metcalf was another person who wasn't afraid of Nellie. He wasn't like the other newsmen Nellie knew. Most of them felt uneasy around her. She was the most important reporter in the nation's most important city. Besides, she wasn't very friendly. She kept them, and most others, at a distance.

Like Nellie, Jim Metcalf was well known in the news world. He was the editor of a national magazine called *Life*. As with Nellie's writing, *Life* caused some readers to feel discomfort or alarm. But it did it in a different way. It revealed the wrongs in society through humor. In articles and cartoons, it poked fun at those who were rich and powerful.

Like his magazine, Jim was humorous, young, and lively. A lock of blonde hair fell over his forehead. He would brush it away, peer at Nellie through steel-rimmed spectacles. He would pretend to be serious.

"Miss Bly," he might say. "You are suffering from a bad case of social reformism. It's likely to be catching. I think we must send you away. How about to Washington, D.C.? *Nobody* can reform anybody *there.*"

Mrs. Cochrane seemed to enjoy Jim's humor more than Nellie did. In fact, Mrs. Cochrane laughed more easily than her daughter did. Nellie's mind was usually on her work. She didn't seem willing to take the *time* to laugh. She didn't even seem willing to take time to think about Jim's being in love with her.

Still, Nellie liked Jim a lot. She liked talking with him, whether he was joking or serious. She admired his work, different as it was from hers. And she was attracted by his good looks, too. All the same, Nellie told her mother, "I don't want to be tied down to any man."

"Besides," she added one day, when she and Mrs. Cochrane were discussing Jim. "Besides—Jim's not a bit like Father."

Mrs. Cochrane raised her eyebrows. "What of it?"

"Well, I—" Nellie felt confused. "If I married anybody—mind you, I don't want to! But if I ever did . . . Well, he'd have to measure up to Father."

Mrs. Cochrane stared at her daughter in silence. At

last she said: "Your father was a fine man, Elizabeth. But he wasn't perfect." She picked up her sewing and rose from her chair. She gave her daughter a little pat on the shoulder as she left the room. "And you're not perfect either, my dear." She laughed.

No, Mrs. Cochrane was not afraid of Nellie Bly.

But sometimes, she was afraid *for* her. That happened often. It was just about to happen again.

Coming home from work one autumn day, Nellie gave her mother a big hug. Her cheeks flamed with excitement. Her gray eyes danced as they never danced when she looked at Jim Metcalf. "You'll never guess!" she cried.

"Could I just take my headache medicine and lie down before you tell me?" said Mrs. Cochrane.

"Oh, Mother—I'm going to go around the world!"

CHAPTER 7

A Race With Time

These days we think it is an ordinary thing to circle the globe. Even the idea of traveling to the moon doesn't seem so unusual to us. But the world of 1889 was, of course, very different from today's world. It was a world with no planes, no automobiles. There were trains, but not everywhere. In some places, there were not even any stagecoaches.

Travel, therefore, was slow. Besides that, it was often difficult, sometimes even dangerous. Few people traveled outside their own countries, much less around the world. So when Nellie announced her plans, her mother said faintly:

"Oh, no, Elizabeth. You're *not.*"

"That's just what Mr. Pulitzer said, at first!" Nellie laughed with delight. "I've been working on him for a whole year. Today, he said yes!"

"Never mind Mr. Pulitzer! I'm your *mother.* And *I* say—"

But Nellie wasn't listening. She gave her mother another hug. "I only came home to tell you the news, Mother. I have to dash right out again. So much to do! I leave in three days."

*

Since childhood, Nellie had liked to read about far-away places. Her favorite book was *Around the World in Eighty Days*, published in 1872. This book, by French writer Jules Verne, was about a character called Phileas Fogg. Phileas made a bet that he could circle the globe in eighty days. Phileas won the bet.

Around the World wasn't a true story. Nobody had ever gone around the world as fast as Phileas. Nobody believed it could be done. That was what gave Nellie her idea. Her idea was that she could *beat* Phileas' record— and see the world while doing it.

At first, Mr. Pulitzer wouldn't listen seriously to Nellie's idea. But she went on talking about it. Little by little, he began to think about it. "Everything has to be tried for the first time," he thought. "Otherwise, there would be no progress. And the *World*'s job is to bring about progress."

"All right. You may try it!" Mr. Pulitizer said at last. "However, we'll send a man with you. Not a reporter, of course. It's *your* reports we want."

"Then why send a man with me? To protect me?" Nellie frowned. "Who protects me in New York?"

"It's not the same. Far more dangerous. You will be in places where women do not go about alone—"

"Hah! Like Mexico!" Nellie cried. A new idea struck her. "If *you* won't send me alone, Mr. Pulitzer, another paper will!"

Mr. Pulitzer gave in. He didn't want to lose Nellie— or the chance for a story that might make history. In fact, now *he* was in a hurry. Nellie had already planned the route she would take. The *World*, Mr. Pulitzer said, could arrange quickly for her passport, visas, tickets. "How fast can you leave?"

"In one day," Nellie said. "Make it three," Mr. Pulitzer said. "What about your clothes? You'll be gone a long time. How will you carry all you'll need?"

"Leave that to me," Nellie said.

It wasn't easy for a woman to travel light, a hundred years ago. Dresses were long and bulky, with bustles. Underclothes were bulky, too. Adding to these problems, Nellie needed clothes for hot climates and cold. Most women would have required a large, heavy trunk.

But Nellie was going to race against time—alone. Whatever she took, she had to carry herself. A trunk would never do.

As soon as Nellie left her mother, she went to a dressmaker. She ordered two dresses: one in heavy blue cloth, one in thin yellow silk. The dressmaker promised to make them in two days. Another customer had not wanted a coat that was already made. It was Nellie's size. It was checked, with a high, warm collar. There was a matching cap, with a bill in front and back. Nellie bought this odd-looking travel cap, too.

Next, Nellie bought a piece of hand luggage called a gripsack. Into this, she crammed her silk dress, a bathrobe, underwear, toilet articles, and writing materials. She put her sewing kit and handkerchiefs into her large purse. Her thin silk raincoat could be carried over her arm.

Nellie's passport and money were in a pouch hung around her neck. But the most important items Nellie carried were two watches. One was a twenty-four hour watch, set to New York time. The other was a watch to be set to the time where she traveled.

Nellie set sail from Hoboken, New Jersey, on November 14, 1889. The day was windy, cold and gray. Nellie had now determined to round the world in seventy-five days. Her ship, the *Augusta Victoria*, left port at three seconds past 9:40 a.m.

Watching Nellie as she boarded the ship were her mother and Jim Metcalf. A few *World* reporters were also on hand. Everyone shouted, "Good luck!" in the wind. Mrs. Cochrane clutched Jim's arm. "Will she ever come back, do you think?" she whispered.

"Why, of course!" he said. But he felt worried. How small Nellie looked on the gangplank! Then Nellie turned. Pulling off her cap, she gaily waved it. "January 27, 1890!" she shouted.

Nellie's jolly mood didn't last long. By noon she was very seasick. So were most of the other passengers. The ship had run into storms. When Nellie wasn't throwing up, she was worrying. Unlike the other passengers, she wasn't worried about drowning. She was worried that the stormy weather would delay the ship.

Nellie's race called for her to go first to London. From there she was to go to Paris, and then to Brindisi, Italy. From that port, she was to sail for the Suez Canal, Egypt. Afterward, it was on to Ceylon (Sri Lanka), Singapore, Hong Kong, and Japan. From Japan, she would sail to San Francisco. Then she had to cross the United States by train, to return to New Jersey.

If she missed some ships or trains, she might lose her race. So even when she got over being seasick, she was still worried.

Meanwhile, the *World* broke the story of Nellie's venture. "AROUND THE WORLD," the headline screamed. "Can Jules Verne's Great Dream Be Reduced to Actual Fact?"

Despite the storms, Nellie's ship was on schedule. In six-and-a-half days, it docked at Southampton, England. There, Nellie was met by the *World*'s London correspondent. "We have a wire from Jules Verne," he said. "He and his wife want to meet you. It would mean a side trip, in France."

Nellie gasped excitedly, "Can it be done? Is there time?"

"You'd have to go back and forth without a night in bed."

"I don't care about that!" Nellie said. So, with the *World* correspondent, she ran to catch her train to London.

In London, Nellie sent a long cable to the *World*. It was her first story about her trip. (There was no way, in those days, to cable from ship to shore.) Then, saying goodbye to the London reporter, she caught another train. It took her to the boat which crossed the English Channel to France. Another train—and she was shaking hands with Mr. and Mrs. Verne.

Jules Verne, his wife, and Nellie all enjoyed their

time together. Nellie showed them the route she meant to take around the world. It was almost the exact route taken by Phileas Fogg. "To think that I should live to see this!" said Mr. Verne. "To see a *woman* make this dream come true," said his wife.

"No, I think it's not yet possible," Jules Verne said. "But your attempt is brave! With my heart, I hope it will succeed!"

"It will, I promise you," said Nellie. Then she was off again, in a horse and buggy, racing to catch her train. Settling down in a second train, to Brindisi, she wrote about her visit with the Vernes. She glanced often at her watch. She'd lost time—and the train was running late. Would she miss her ship?

But at Brindisi, her new ship, the *Victoria*, was still in port. Nellie hurried on board. There, she learned that the ship would not sail for two hours. Back to land she rushed, to find a cable office. She sent the *World* the good news that she had reached the *Victoria*. "Leaving now for Suez!" said her cable.

Aboard again, Nellie caught up on her sleep. When she woke, the ship was in the blue-and-purple waters of the Mediterranean Sea. It was calm. Nellie wasn't seasick. She had never felt better.

She began to enjoy herself. There were ship parties, music, and dancing. Nellie made friends among her shipmates, mostly English people. They didn't know who she was, and she didn't tell them. To them, she was "that pretty Miss Cochrane." Maybe a bit strange, they thought. She seemed to own only two gowns!

But elsewhere, Nellie Bly's name was on everyone's lips. Every paper in the U.S., and many in other countries, had stories about her travels. Readers of the *World* followed her progress daily. The paper had started a Nellie Bly Guessing Game Contest. Thousands of readers sent in their bets on the exact time of Nellie's return. The prize was a free trip to Europe and $250.

As this excitement raged at home, Nellie reached Port Said, Egypt. There was disease there, so most of the passengers stayed on the ship. But Nellie hired a donkey to ride through the town. The poverty here was the worst she'd ever seen. Men and boys fought for the few pennies they earned as guides. Beggars were everywhere. Hungry children roamed in the dirt of the streets.

Moved by pity and anger, Nellie felt helpless. Her reports on this place, she knew, weren't likely to lead to reforms. As the *Victoria* crawled through the Suez Canal, Nellie was in low spirits. She wrote that the Canal looked like a dirty ditch.

Her spirits sank even lower when the *Victoria* fell behind schedule. It was two days late when it steamed into Colombo, Ceylon. But this was not the end of the delays.

Nellie's next ship, the *Oriental*, was waiting in port. But that was *all* it was doing. It was waiting for passengers and mail from another ship. There was no sign of this ship, reported to be a leaky old tub. Nellie was stuck.

She remained stuck until December 15. Then the

leaky tub showed up. The *Oriental* got underway—but Nellie had lost five days. She felt somewhat relieved when the ship reached Singapore. Only forty-one days were left for her journey. But with luck, she could still make it.

Her luck held until she reached Hong Kong. In spite of rough weather, the *Oriental* docked there on December 22. Nellie swung cheerfully into the office of her new steamship line. On her shoulder was a small monkey she had bought in Singapore. An official of the steamship line shook her hand.

"Glad to see you looking so well," he said. "We thought you might be upset."

"Upset?"

"Why, yes, about that other girl. The one who's going around the world, in the opposite direction? She started the day after you did. She's already four days ahead of you."

Rags to Riches

"Surely," Nellie said, "you are joking?"

"Why, no," the official said. "I wouldn't do that!"

Nellie's face had become pale. She felt as if the ground had crumbled under her feet. She said, "How do you know about this—this other traveler?"

"Her name is Miss Bisland. She came to Hong Kong on our ship, from San Francisco. She left for Singapore four days ago!"

Nellie hurried to pick up her messages. She had a number of cables from the *World*. None said anything about Miss Bisland. "Well," Nellie thought, "the *World* isn't paying any attention to Miss Bisland. So I won't, either."

But her heart was heavy as she toured Hong Kong. Her shipmates tried to cheer her up. By now, they all knew who she was. "If it weren't for you, no one would be trying such a race," they said. "It was your idea. And you will win, too!"

Nellie took a side trip to Canton, China, where she visted a prison. She saw the machines used to punish lawbreakers by torture. "Poor souls!" she thought. Thinking of such misery made her ashamed to be worrying about the race. In a sober mood she returned to Hong Kong, on Christmas Eve.

Three days later, her ship sailed for Yokohama, Japan. On January 3, it arrived there. A crowd of Japanese reporters greeted Nellie.

Around the World in Eighty Days was well known in Japan, in translation. The Japanese were great fans of Jules Verne. Nellie's story of her visit with him had been translated into Japanese. It had appeared in newspapers all over Japan. So had many news reports about Nellie's journey. She had become famous in Japan. Wherever she went, an eager crowd followed her.

Nellie had not known, until now, how big a stir her journey was making. She hadn't heard about the Guessing Game. The Japanese were playing it, too. They were also singing—in English—an American song that had been written about her trip.

The Japanese were charmed by Nellie. And Nellie was charmed by the Japanese. Her reports from Japan bubbled with praise. The Japanese, she wrote, were a graceful people. Their houses and streets were the cleanest she'd ever seen. Their children were healthy and happy-looking. Yokohama and Tokyo, the capital, were cheerful cities—not like Canton or Port Said!

Four days was all the time Nellie had to spend in Japan. Then her ship sailed for home, from Yokohama. The city gave her a wonderful send-off. She was showered with gifts and flowers. The crowd shouted, waved, and wept. Drums banged, gongs sounded, steamship whistles blew. The band played "Home

Sweet Home."

Nellie had almost forgotten Miss Bisland. Nobody had said a word about her in Japan. Or, if so, it wasn't translated. Besides, Nellie had reached the next-to-last leg of her journey.

But on the third day out, the ship met bad weather. It was the worst storm that winter. As the ship tossed and rolled, Nellie counted every hour. "If we don't make port in ten days, I'm finished," she told the captain.

"Where's that monkey of yours?" the captain asked.

"The last time I saw him, he was hiding under my bunk. He's afraid of the storm," Nellie said. "But why do you ask?"

"Sailors believe a monkey is bad luck on a ship. They think the storm might stop if they threw him overboard." At the horrified look on Nellie's face, the captain laughed. "I don't think they'd do it. Still, it's just as well he's in hiding."

But the crew was really rooting for Nellie. In the engine room, someone had put up a sign that said:

For Nellie Bly
We'll do or die!
January 20, 1890

They did not make port by that date. But with skillful work, the ship was in sight of San Francisco on January 21. Only in sight, however. For now there was another hitch.

A rumor had started that there was smallpox among the passengers. And the ship's bill of health was missing. It looked as if everyone must be kept aboard for an indefinite time.

Frantic, Nellie cried, "Put me ashore, or I'll swim ashore!"

The captain saw no good reason to refuse Nellie. He knew the ship had been given a clean bill of health before it left Yokohama. And the San Francisco quarantine doctor had already examined Nellie. So the captain sent her ashore in a launch.

San Francisco was covered in early morning fog as the launch bumped the dock. Nellie stepped ashore. Her heart was beating fast. "Home," she thought. "I'm *home!*" Monkey on her shoulder, gripsack in hand, she entered the waiting room.

A din burst out as she came through the door. There were shouts and cheers. "It's Nellie Bly! Nellie is home! Hooray for Nellie Bly!" It looked as though all of San Francisco was jammed into the room. A band struck up "Hail Columbia."

The Mayor of San Francisco made a brief speech. Then Nellie was asked to speak. Tears in her eyes, she said: "For sixty-eight days I've been dashing around the world and . . . there's no place like home!" She pulled off her cap and waved it.

Then Nellie had to dash once more. Her race was not won. She had a week, at most, to cross the country, and the weather was bad along her route. Blizzards were stopping many trains.

A parade formed to escort Nellie to the train station. It included city officials, suffragists, marching bands, and hundreds of other San Franciscans. Reporters swarmed around the special railway car prepared for Nellie. It was decked with banners. Her name was painted on it, in gold letters.

At every stop on Nellie's route, people were waiting to greet her. Everyone wanted to see the famous Nellie Bly, in her famous checked cap. They wanted to see the monkey, who was now in the news, too. Where there was no stop, people stood along the tracks, to watch her train go by. They held up banners: "NOTHING CAN STOP NELLIE!" and "NELLIE BLY WILL WIN!"

The weather didn't seem to want Nellie to win. Because of snowstorms, she could not take a direct route. This meant losing time. But her trains managed to make up the time. On January 25, Nellie began to feel sure she would make her target. That was when she changed to her last train, in Philadelphia.

Waiting for her there in her special railway car were some special people. They had come from New York to make the final short run with her. Her mother and Jim Metcalf were there, along with Julius Chambers, her editor at the *World*.

Mrs. Cochrane cried with joy. But she wasn't overjoyed to meet the monkey. Accepting its paw, she said, "One of us is going to the zoo. And I don't think it's going to be me."

While everyone was laughing and talking, Nellie

spoke to her *World* editor. In a low voice, she said, "And what about Miss Bisland?" Chambers said, "What? You heard about that?" He laughed. "She was stuck somewhere in Europe, last I heard. She's a magazine writer, not a news reporter." He looked hard at Nellie. "Don't tell me you've been *worrying!*"

Nellie didn't answer. She wasn't worrying *now,* anyway. She even began to feel a little proud about Miss Bisland. "After all," she thought, "I wanted to show women what they can do!"

Nellie's last stop was Jersey City. That was where her final time would be clocked. On either side of the tracks, as the train drew near, Nellie saw crowds waiting. The station was packed with thousands of people as she sprang to the platform. The time-keeper shouted: *"Seventy-two days, six hours, ten minutes, and eleven seconds!"*

A roar went up from the crowd. Nellie had not only beaten Phileas Fogg, an imaginary person. Traveling 24,899 miles to circle the globe, she had outdone every record in history.

"From Jersey back to Jersey!" Nellie cried. Her gray eyes sparkled. Her cap, now battered, waved once more in the air.

When Nellie got to New York, ten guns boomed a salute. In an open carriage, she moved through cheering crowds to the *World* office. There she was welcomed by the mayor, the governor, and—most important to her—Joseph Pulitzer.

Under a banner headline, "FATHER TIME OUT-

DONE!" the whole front page of the next day's *World* was given to Nellie. Even today, articles about women seldom appear on the front page. When they do, the women are often the wives of important men or the victims of crimes. But papers all over the world carried front-page stories on Nellie's victory. Messages of praise poured in, too—from the city of Pittsburgh, from Jules Verne, from great scientists and explorers.

The excitement was as great as that caused by the first successful space travel years later. For Nellie's fast trip seemed just as impossible to people at that time, until she tried it.

Soon after Nellie's return, she set out on a cross-country lecture tour. Both her mother and Jim Metcalf protested. "You just came *back!*" said Jim. And Mrs. Cochrane said: "I won't be left here to look after that monkey!" With a sigh, Nellie kissed the monkey goodbye. She turned it over to the zoo. Then she kissed Jim and her mother goodbye—and was gone.

Lectures in those days were a popular form of entertainment and education. They were as popular as TV is now. People flocked to see and hear Nellie. They were thrilled by her stories of faraway lands and peoples. They were amazed that this small person had braved storms, disease, and discomfort.

Nellie found time to write a book about her travels. It was published in 1890 and was a best seller. She had earlier published two other books—one about Mexico, another about Blackwell's Island asylum. The sales of these now increased.

Suddenly, Nellie was a wealthy woman. Her books and lectures made money. Her work at the *World,* and columns in other papers, brought in more. Nellie's income shot up to $25,000 a year. That was a fortune in the 1890s, especially for a woman.

Sometimes Elizabeth Cochrane could hardly believe that she was Nellie Bly. It wasn't long ago that she had been worrying about how to pay the rent. She had gone from near-rags to riches. She had gone from pleading at locked doors to fame.

At twenty-six, she was known on every continent. In the United States, the public adored her. Song after song was written about her. A race horse was named after her. Her clothes and hairstyle were copied. Nellie Bly travel caps were manufactured and worn by the thousands. Nellie's name and image appeared in ads for soap, cigars, and chewing gum.

In Mrs. Cochrane's opinion, however, fame and fortune weren't everything. "You know, Elizabeth," she said, "you really should start thinking about getting married."

"Goodness me," said Nellie "What on earth for?"

Her eyes shone. She was having the time of her life.

CHAPTER 9

Goodbye, Miss Bly

Yes, Nellie was enjoying her new fame and fortune. But that wasn't the only reason she was in no hurry to marry. Nellie also wanted to be free—free to do as she pleased.

She had struggled hard for her freedom. She had been told, over and over, that she couldn't do what she wanted to. She had been told that she couldn't be a reporter. She'd been told that she couldn't write about certain subjects. She'd been told that she couldn't go here and shouldn't go there.

And why? Because she was a woman.

Nellie had not let that stop her. Each time someone had said "no," she had pushed ahead. She had pushed through locked doors. She had put up with being laughed at. She had not been stopped by fear, and she had not been stopped by criticism.

But what if she had been *married*? Nellie thought. Was it likely that she could have had the same success? Even women who were single were kept out of "men's work." They had to fight to become lawyers, doctors, printers, musicians. Only a few won.

But it was still worse for women who were married.

Often, when a woman married, she was fired from whatever job she had. Employers thought that a woman would not work very hard, with a husband to support her. As for the kind of freedom Nellie had, most married women didn't dream of it. Even more than single women, married women were expected to stay quietly at home.

Nellie didn't want to stay quietly at home. She wanted to play a part in what went on in the world. She wasn't ready to give that up for marriage. "Maybe . . . *someday,*" she thought.

Nellie's lecture tour lasted nine months. As soon as she returned, she plunged into more work.

This was a time of deep trouble in the nation. The rich were getting richer as the poor grew poorer. Immigrants, encouraged to come to the United States as cheap labor, swelled the urban slums. There were labor strikes, put down with violence. Crime increased. Crooked politics continued.

At the same time, a wave of reform was sweeping the country. Nellie joined the *World* in the battle for reform. She toured the New York slums, reporting on the outbreak of disease. She risked her health there as she had in Port Said. She interviewed poor women who made a living as thieves or prostitutes. She went into homes for the aged and wrote about how badly they were cared for.

Some of Nellie's most important stories were written in 1894-95. By then, the United States was in the grip of a very bad depression. Millions were out of work. People roamed the country, looking for jobs.

In 1894, there was a big railroad strike, centered in Chicago. It started after the Pullman railway car company cut wages, some as much as forty percent. The Pullman workers and their families were all but starving. When a committee of workers begged Mr. Pullman for a better deal, he wouldn't listen. So, with the help of the American Railway Union, the workers went on strike.

George Pullman hired thugs to break up the strike. The President himself sent federal troops to Chicago to get the trains moving. When the troops arrived, there was a riot in the rail yards. Some railroad cars were burned. The strikers were blamed for everything. Eugene V. Debs, head of the American Railway Union, was thrown into jail. The strike was crushed.

Newspapers throughout the nation heaped harsh words on the strikers. Yet no one really knew how the riot had started. And almost nothing was known about the strikers or the reasons for the strike. So Nellie, with the *World*'s backing, set out to investigate.

She went to the small, Illinois country town where Eugene V. Debs was in jail. Pretending to be a friend of his, she got in to interview him. "I'm Nellie Bly," she whispered to Debs.

Newspapers had described Debs as a wild radical who had encouraged the strikers to riot. To Nellie's surprise, Debs' "jail" was a room at the back of the sheriff's house. His guard was the sheriff's wife. She didn't seem to be afraid of Debs. In fact, the lock on his door was in need of repair.

"The other night I had to lock myself in," Debs told Nellie with a chuckle.

Tall and lean, with a craggy face, Debs was gentle and kind. Nellie's story showed that Debs was not the kind of man to encourage violence. "His belief," she told her surprised readers, "is in the religion of the Golden Rule. I don't know of any man who would make a better leader for any class of people."

His mission is a decent wage for railroad workers. He saw that all the railroads were coming together, and that they mean to reduce wages, first one place and then another. This is what Eugene Debs was working against.

Nellie also visited the Pullman workers and their families. They lived in a town built and owned by Mr. Pullman. The town, near Chicago, was supposed to be run for the workers' benefit. But Nellie found out that this was not the case.

The town store charged high prices for food and goods. Rents were high, too. "Did Mr. Pullman lower the rents when he cut wages?" Nellie asked. "He did not," said the workers. Their wives said: "Prices for food are still high. We can't feed our children. Just scraps. Not one real meal a day."

Nellie saw the hungry, ragged children. She saw the bare, cheerless homes. She saw despair. She saw it all, and reported it firsthand.

As always, Nellie searched *behind* events to find out

what was really going on. Sometimes she did this by using a disguise. Sometimes she did it by getting people to confide in her. One way or another, she got at the truths behind the news.

This kind of reporting was Nellie's main contribution to journalism. Today people call it "investigative reporting." It had not often been done by reporters before Nellie's time.

Searching for her firsthand stories, Nellie left New York more and more often. She was always getting on and off trains. She saw her mother less. She saw less and less of Jim Metcalf.

One winter night she sat talking with Jim in front of her own fireplace. Nellie wore a blue velvet evening dress with a wide sash. Metcalf was also in evening clothes. They had been to the opera with Mrs. Cochrane, who had just gone to bed.

"Off again tomorrow, then?" said Jim.

Nellie nodded. "For the wild West. Morning train."

Jim took her hand. "Nellie, have you noticed that I am growing old and gray and stooped?"

Nellie laughed. "You look about the same to me."

"Well, I *feel* that I've grown old and gray, waiting for you. Nellie, truthfully—do you ever intend to marry me?"

"I can't promise that I will," Nellie said. "I never *said* I would. I just don't know."

"By now," Jim said, "you'd know a little more, if you cared more for me." He squeezed her hand, then dropped it. "I just can't go on dangling, Nellie. To tell the truth, it hurts too much. I think we shouldn't meet any more."

He got to his feet. Nellie rose, too. "I'm sorry," she said. "You know, I'm really very fond of you."

They walked to the door. "I *am* fond of you," Nellie said. "I'll miss you, Jim."

He smiled. "Perhaps. Goodbye, Miss Bly. That makes a passable rhyme, doesn't it? Too bad I can't use it in *Life*."

The door closed behind him.

Mrs. Cochrane was not happy to hear that Nellie and Jim had parted. Nellie was now thirty. Mrs. Cochrane began to lose hope that Nellie was ever going to get married.

Just as Mrs. Cochrane was giving up hope, Nellie met her future husband, on a train. Five days later, she married him.

Robert Seaman was a self-made man. He owned a factory and had long been a millionaire. He was a bachelor, and handsome.

He was also seventy-two years old when Nellie met him.

Afraid of almost nothing, Nellie was afraid of how her mother would take this marriage. She sent the news to her mother by wire, from Chicago. That was where Nellie and Seaman had left the train together. They were married there, on April 5, 1895.

Nellie wrote to Mrs. Cochrane about Robert Seaman: "He's *wonderful*! Interesting, successful—a lot like Father!"

When Mrs. Cochrane met Seaman, she thought: "He's too *old* to be her father. *Grandfather's* more like it!"

She had to admit that Seaman was, except for age, a match for her unusual daughter. He *was* an interesting person. He had seen much more of the world than Nellie. He knew much more, although he was self-educated. It was also clear that he loved Nellie and had respect for her strength and talent.

Yet Mrs. Cochrane never quite forgave Nellie for marrying Seaman. Nellie, in turn, was hurt by her mother's disapproval. From that time on, the bond between them weakened.

Mrs. Cochrane was not alone in her disapproval. Nellie's public was shocked. Surely, people thought, their dashing Nellie deserved a more romantic match! In the newspaper world, there was also disapproval. Nellie was called a fortune hunter for marrying a rich old man. "What will he do—hobble after her, around the world?" everyone said. "It won't work out!"

But everyone was wrong. First of all, Nellie retired. The comet of her career, blazing for ten years, suddenly went out. She and Seaman did go around the world together. They went often. They took their time. They went to the museums, gardens, and concerts Nellie had missed in her hasty global dash.

In New York they lived in Seaman's large, beautiful

house. There Nellie met people in Seaman's circle. She enjoyed their company. Like Seaman, most of them were smart and interesting. Nellie also took an interest in Seaman's factory, where hardware was made. It was not like the dreadful factories Nellie had exposed. Nellie approved of the wages and conditions.

If Nellie sometimes thought, "Too *tame!*" nobody knew it. For nearly ten years, she seemed content. Then Seaman died.

Nellie took over the factory. For a while she did very well; she even expanded business. Then things began to go wrong.

An employee invested money from the business and lost it. He claimed that he was acting under Nellie's orders. Nellie sued him. He counter-sued her. Next, one of the factory buildings burned down. There were problems about the insurance. Nellie sued the insurance company. Then customers whose orders weren't being filled sued Nellie.

Seaman's millions were eaten up by lawsuits. To escape her creditors, Nellie fled to Europe. When she boarded the ship, both her fortune and Seaman's were nearly gone.

All the same, this time she took a trunk full of clothes.

The Last Big Story

Nellie set sail on a beautiful day in July, 1914. She did not intend to be away for very long. She had left her affairs in the hands of a good lawyer. She felt sure that he would be able to clear things up with her creditors.

Meanwhile she could manage, Nellie thought. In Austria, where she planned to stay, she could live well on little money. As the shores of New York faded, she turned from the rail with a smile. She would see those shores again soon, she thought.

Nellie was wrong about all of this. Her lawyer did not clear things up quickly. And one month after Nellie left, the First World War broke out. Nellie was still in Austria when the United States entered the war. She remained stranded there until the war's end, with just enough money to get by.

She returned to New York in 1919. The lawyer had not been able to work any magic. At the age of fifty-five, Nellie was broke.

Fortunately, she still had the means to earn a living. She didn't want to return to the *World*, however. Mr. Pulitzer had died years before. Almost no one Nellie knew was still working at the *World*.

In Austria, Nellie had written some reports on the war for the New York *Evening Journal.* She went now to see the *Journal*'s editor, Arthur Brisbane, and asked him for a job.

"Why, Nellie," Brisbane said, "that would be a pleasure. The *Journal* would be honored to have you as a reporter."

Brisbane and Nellie had been at the *World* together. Like so many others, he admired Nellie's talents. He knew she would do a first-class job as a reporter.

Still, as he looked at her, he felt troubled. Behind the veil of her pretty hat, Nellie's face was tired. There was almost no trace of the dashing young reporter Brisbane remembered. In this busy newspaper office, she looked out of place, Brisbane thought.

And . . . "old-fashioned," he thought. During the war, women's fashions had changed. Skirts were shorter; garments were looser, more comfortable. But Nellie wore a tight, formal-looking jacket and a skirt that swept the floor. Her slightly outdated look gave Brisbane a sad feeling. He felt that Nellie didn't really want to enter the modern world.

It was a new, fast-paced world, in which Nellie's fame had faded. Her dash around the globe no longer seemed so amazing. Transportation had speeded up. Automobiles had replaced slow, horse-drawn carriages in the city streets. Even airplanes had come into use since the war.

Nellie's daring deeds didn't seem so unusual for a woman now, either. Women had gained more freedom to come and go as they pleased. Many more women held paid jobs, too. And more and more, they had fought their way into "men's work." That included newspaper work.

If Nellie was a strange sight at the *Journal*, it wasn't because she was a woman. Other women worked there—although men still greatly outnumbered them, especially as reporters.

Wearing a hat with a heavy veil, Nellie arrived each day at the *Journal*. Out of his old respect for her, Brisbane gave her a private office. There she worked, her door closed.

The women who worked at the *Journal* didn't pay much attention to Nellie. To them, she was just a strange lady in a fancy hat. They didn't know that she had opened a path for women reporters. They didn't know about the time when women weren't seen in newspaper offices. Nellie could have told them a lot about that. But she never talked to them.

In the old days, Nellie hadn't been very friendly with her male co-workers. Now she didn't try to make friends with the women, either. With their youth and energy, they made her feel like a ghost of her former self. So she did her work and drew her pay, speaking to almost no one except Brisbane.

But Nellie still cared about the world she lived in. She still wanted to make it a better place. She told Brisbane she wanted to write a regular column about the poor children in New York. She took up the cause of abandoned children, using her column to find homes for them.

Nellie still wrote stories of her own choosing, such as those on the children. But she also covered events assigned by Brisbane. One day he called her into his office.

"Are you interested in capital punishment, Nellie?" asked Brisbane.

"I'm very much against it," Nellie said. "It's wrong for a person to kill. But it's wrong for the government to take that person's life, too. That's just legalized murder."

"There are some who agree with you," said Brisbane. "A number of groups are trying to put an end to the death penalty."

"I know," Nellie said. "They've tried to stop the execution of Gordon Hamby. But it's going to happen, anyway."

"That's what I want to talk about," said Brisbane. "I plan to send a reporter to cover Hamby's execution." He hesitated and then went on. "Do you want the assignment?"

Nellie was silent. She knew that she could refuse. And she wanted to refuse. Gordon Hamby was a convicted murderer, but she didn't want to see him die. She didn't want to watch any human being die in the electric chair.

And yet, she thought, it would be wrong to say no. Wrong, because her story might help to end the death penalty. *Her* story—*more* than someone else's. Although she felt old and tired, Nellie still believed in the power of her writing. So she agreed to take the assignment.

As she had expected, it was a nightmare to watch the execution. Her story reflected pain and horror. It was a strong protest against capital punishment.

Nellie's eyewitness account of an execution was not the very first. But it was rare. No woman had seen an execution in New York State for twenty-nine years. The *Journal* ran the story in its front pages, under a bold headline.

It was Nellie's last big story. It came toward the end of her life. Two years later, in January 1922, Nellie died of pneumonia, at a New York hospital. She was fifty-seven.

She had lived alone, at a hotel, since her return from Austria. She was out of touch with her mother and had no close friends. Sometimes she took in an abandoned child, but only until a real home could be found. Very few people attended her funeral.

Her death didn't make a big splash in the newspapers. The *World* carried the longest story. It told of her race around the world. It recalled her exposé of Blackwell's Island asylum and other crusades. The *Pittsburgh Dispatch*, where she got her start, boasted that Nellie "was considered the best reporter in America." But some newspapers did not note her passing at all.

Yet newspapers, and the country, owed Nellie a debt. She had used the power of the press to uncover many wrongs. She had used her talent as a writer to help correct them.

Always questioning, Nellie had led others to question. She questioned the idea that women are tender, frail plants, best kept in the house. With daring and courage, she set out to destroy that myth. By her example, she helped women dream of a world in which they might be free.

That world was taking shape in 1922, when Nellie died. Women's right to vote had been written into the U.S. Constitution in 1920. By then, there were a number of reforms in the conditions of working women in factories. Divorce laws had also become more favorable to women in this period. There was progress in many causes that Nellie had taken to heart.

Nellie herself was nearly forgotten as the years passed after her death. After a while, most people did not even know that "Nellie Bly" had been the pen name of a real person. They thought it was only the name of an old song.

It was not until nearly sixty years after her death that Nellie's memory was honored. By that time women, who had been quiet for some years as a group, had once again formed a strong movement. This modern feminist movement sparked a new respect for women's work and history. In 1978, the New York Press Club raised a monument over Nellie's grave, reading, "To Nellie Bly, A Famous News Reporter."

There is more interest now in what Nellie Bly accomplished. In her day, Nellie had to beat down doors to become a reporter. Today's newswomen have also had to struggle for a chance at "men's jobs," such as news editor, sports reporter, and TV anchor. Nellie wrote story after story about the problems of women and children. The special problems of today's women and children have only lately had serious notice in the news. Above all, Nellie helped lead the way in investigative reporting—a search for truth that some are still carrying on.

Nellie Bly's star rose rapidly and set in her own lifetime. As women search now for the truths of their history, her star begins to climb again.

IDA B. WELLS

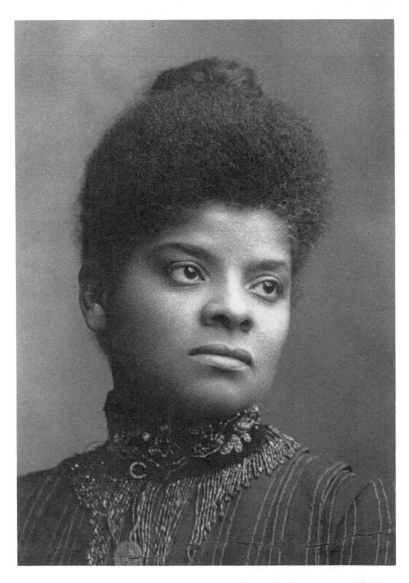

In 1893, Ida B. Wells went to Great Britain to gain support for her crusade against lynching. By then she was well-known to readers of African-American newspapers.

Autumn 1896. Ida B. Wells with her firstborn son, Charles Aked Barnett. Ida took the baby with her when traveling to meetings.

December 1917 during World War I. There were frequent race riots in this period. Ida B. Wells' newspaper reports on the riots provided badly needed facts.

Outline of Life Events

July 16, 1862: Ida Bell Wells born in Holly Springs, Mississippi.

1878-83: After parents die of yellow fever, supports five sisters and brothers by teaching school.

1883-84: Moves to Memphis, Tennessee. Teaches school and attends Fisk University. Sues railroad in discrimination case. Publishes first article, about her suit, in a black church paper.

1884-91: Under pen name "Iola," writes for African-American newspapers nation-wide. Becomes editor and part-owner of weekly, *Free Speech and Headlight.* Loses teaching job for writing about bad conditions in black schools. Becomes fulltime journalist.

1892: Three black Memphis men lynched. Demands justice in *Free Speech.* Begins investigation of lynchings. Attacks forbidden topic of black-on-white rape as myth used to justify lynching.

1892-94: White mob destroys *Free Speech.* Moves to New York, taking job with the *New York Age.* Begins one-woman anti-lynching crusade. Publishes *Southern Horrors.* Speaking tours in U.S. and Great Britain. With

Frederick Douglass, publishes book on achievements of black Americans. Starts Chicago's first black women's club.

1895-1900: Marries Ferdinand Lee Barnett, Chicago lawyer and publisher, **1895.** Edits weekly, *The Conservator.* First two children born: Charles, **1896**; Herman, **1897.** Helps found National Association of Colored Women's Clubs and National Afro-American Council. Continues anti-lynching crusade.

1901-17: Ida, Jr., born, **1901**; Alfreda born, **1904.** Helps found National Association for the Advancement of Colored People, **1909.** Starts Negro Fellowship League, a shelter/employment center for black Southern migrants. Founds Alpha Suffrage Club for black women. Marches in suffrage parades in Chicago; Washington, D.C.

1917-29: Investigates anti-black riots that begin during World War I. Travels to East St. Louis and Arkansas to report on riots. Writing and speaking to defend blacks unjustly imprisoned for starting riots, she finally sees them freed. Continues leadership in women's club movement, but loses **1924** race for president of National Association of Colored Women's Clubs.

1929-31: Runs for Illinois state senate as a Republican independent. Supported only by black women and a few organizations, loses in **1930** primary. Dies of uremia, **March 25, 1931**, at the age of sixty-nine.

CHAPTER 1

A Mind of Her Own

In 1990 many people noticed a bright new U.S. postage stamp. On this stamp is the portrait of a woman. She wears a high lace collar, in the style of the early twentieth century. Her blue-black hair is piled high on her head. Her nut-brown skin looks soft, and her lips are smiling. But her big dark eyes flash fire.

The name of this remarkable woman was Ida B. Wells.

Ida B. Wells was born a slave, to slave parents. The date of her birth, in Holly Springs, Mississippi, was July 16, 1862. Three years later, after the Civil War, slavery came to an end.

Ida grew up to be a writer. Her written words led to important changes in history. Yet when she was born, her parents could not write or read. Slaves were not taught to read and write. It was against the law to teach them.

However, by the time Ida was three, there were schools for the former slaves. Ida and her parents, Lizzie and Jim Wells, started school together. Their teachers were white people from the North. These teachers wanted to help the newly freed African-

Americans get ahead. They knew that almost no white Southerners would help them.

In a few years, Ida's mother could read the Bible. Ida's father liked to read newspapers best. So Ida got the idea that the Bible and newspapers were both very important. (She went on thinking that, all her life.) But Ida didn't dream that someday *she* would write for newspapers. She didn't dream that she would become one of America's first women reporters. All that came later on.

Ida's father, a carpenter, started his own business not long after freedom. Her mother had a job as a cook. Together, they saved money and built a house of their own. They had six more children after Ida was born. Ida helped out with the younger children. But she still had time to read and play. Ida's young life was very happy.

Then, when Ida was sixteen, everything changed. Her happy girlhood came to a sudden end.

High up in a plum tree, Ida sat reading. The evening sun, warm and golden, slanted across the pages of her book.

"Ida, Ida! Where are you?"

"Up here, Grandma." Ida leaned out of the tree.

"Almost time for supper."

"I'll help," Ida said. She scrambled out of the tree. Ida and her grandmother crossed the yard together. "Days getting shorter," Grandma Peggy said. "Seems like you just got here. Now it's nearly time for you to leave."

Every summer, Ida visited her grandparents' farm. It was in pretty countryside, fifty miles from Holly Springs. Ida loved being on the farm.

As they drew near the house, three men on horses rode to the gate. The men were friends of Ida's parents, from Holly Springs.

Grandma Peggy asked the men to have a seat on the shady porch. "I'll just get you some cold lemonade," she said. "Then you can tell us the news from Holly Springs. Been a long time since we had a letter."

"Well, ma'am," one of the men said, "we don't have good news. There's yellow fever in Holly Springs. It's been real bad." His face was sad.

He took a piece of paper from his pocket. Handing the paper to Ida, he said, "You best read this, Ida."

Ida read the letter out loud to Grandma Peggy. The first page of the letter told about the yellow fever. The fever had started in Memphis, over the border in Tennessee. Then it spread to Holly Springs.

As Ida read the second page, her voice began to tremble. "Jim and Lizzie Wells have both died of the fever," she read. "The children are all at home. A neighbor is taking care of them. They . . . . "

A cold hand squeezed Ida's throat. She could not go on. The tears were running down Grandma Peggy's face. She put her arms around Ida. Locked together, they stood rocking on the porch. The men began to cry, too.

Now Ida found her voice. "I have to go home,"

she said.

One of the men spoke up. "Ida, everybody who can leave Holly Springs is leaving. Stay here until the fever ends."

Ida shook her head. "My sisters and brothers need me."

"No, no," said Grandma Peggy. "I'm not going to lose you, too! Grandpa and I will go to the children."

"You and Grandpa have to bring in the cotton crop," Ida said. "Cotton won't wait." She looked across the yard and saw the plum tree. The last rays of sun were gilding its top branches. Never again, she knew, would she climb that tree with a girl's light heart.

The next day, Ida was on a train to Holly Springs. At home, she found two of the children in bed with the fever. The youngest child, a baby of nine months, had died. This left sisters of twelve, five, and two years old. There was also a brother of eleven, and one who was nine.

The children were frightened. Ida comforted them and took care of them. Many more people died of yellow fever. But Ida and her five sisters and brothers stayed alive.

When the fever ended, members of Jim Wells' lodge gathered at the Wells' home. The lodge was a group of black men who had banded together for the good of their community. They gave whatever help they could to needy black people. Ida's father had been a leading member of the lodge. Now that he was gone, his lodge brothers wanted to provide for his children. They told

Ida their plans.

They said that they had found homes for each of the four youngest children. Each of them was to be taken in by a different family. But Ida's twelve-year-old sister, badly disabled since birth, needed special care. They had not been able to find a family that would take her. So she would have to go to the poorhouse. And Ida, they said, was old enough now to fend for herself.

Ida said, "I thank you for your trouble, gentlemen. But I'm not going to let the children be scattered. They don't need anybody else's home. *This* is their home. Mama and Papa built it for us. And I'm going to take care of the children myself."

"Why, that's nice, Ida," said one of the men kindly. "But how will you get them food and clothes?"

"I will get a job teaching school," Ida said.

The lodge members looked at Ida. What they saw was a pretty, skinny young girl. Her hair hung in a plait down her back. She wore the short skirts of a child. She didn't look anything like a school teacher.

Still, they knew that Ida was smart. She was always at the top of her class in school. She could probably pass the examination for school teacher.

But more important, Ida was stubborn. What Jim Wells used to say of his daughter was true. Neighbors said it, too. And teachers: "Our Ida has a mind of her own."

So the men didn't argue with Ida. They wished her luck and said goodnight. "You need any help, you let us know," they told Ida.

"Sure will," Ida said. As she shut the door, she thought: "I don't need help to put my sister in the poorhouse!"

Then she thought: "Well, they *did* want to try to help. I ought to watch my temper."

Ida took the teachers' examination. She passed easily. The next thing was to find a job. In Mississippi, school teachers had to be at least eighteen. Ida knew she would have to look older than she was. So she thought up some ways to do that.

First she let down the hem of her best dress. When she tried it on, her sisters and brothers burst out laughing. "Oh, Miz Ida!" they cried. "Oh, *old* Miz Ida!"

Ida took her hair out of its plait. She pinned the hair on top of her head. At first, the hair would not stay up. It kept falling out of the pins. The children laughed even harder at that.

Ida laughed too. She was glad to see the children having a good time. They had been through a lot of sad days.

Ida got a job at a country school. The job paid twenty-five dollars a month. The school was six miles from Holly Springs. Someone would have to stay with the children while Ida was gone. She found an old friend of her mother's to stay during the week.

Ida came home every Friday, riding on the back of a fat mule. On Saturdays and Sundays, she washed and ironed. She also cooked food to be left for the children's weekly meals. Late in the afternoon on Sunday, she would ride back to the country.

Riding through the gathering darkness, Ida sometimes felt lonesome and sad. She had been able to fool people into thinking she was grown up. But often she still felt like a child. She missed her parents. They had petted Ida; they had done most things for her. It was hard to take on so many burdens, so suddenly.

But then Ida would cheer up. She would begin to make plans. She wanted to get more education. She wanted to see more of the world. She didn't plan to teach forever at a country school.

In fact, she stayed at her country school for only a few years. Then, in 1883, she moved to the city of Memphis.

It was there that she found the path she would follow all her life.

CHAPTER 2

Ida Becomes Iola

"Where's my kitty? I won't go without my kitty!"

"Here she is!" Ida put a gray kitten into her sister's arms. "Now—are we ready to go?"

It was a bright June morning. Ida and her two youngest sisters were saying goodbye to Holly Springs. Ida's disabled sister and the two boys had already left. They had gone to live on Aunt Belle's farm. Belle was a sister of Ida's mother. The children were fond of her. Ida knew that they would be well cared for.

Ida and the two little girls were going to Memphis, Tennessee. Aunt Fannie Butler, who lived in Memphis, had asked Ida to move there. It seemed like a good idea. Ida would be able to get a better-paid teaching job. Aunt Fannie would care for the children.

Aunt Fannie had a big, comfortable house. She welcomed the children—and the kitten, too. Ida's little sisters soon felt at home.

By autumn, Ida had a new job. It was at a country school, about fifty miles from Memphis. Ida spent weekends in Memphis with Aunt Fannie and the children. Then, on Sundays, she returned to her country school. But she didn't ride a mule. She rode on the train. With her hair tucked under a small hat, and her neat gloves, she was a smart-looking figure.

One day in May of 1884, Ida was on the train. She sat reading a book, as usual. When the conductor came to her seat, she held out her ticket. "I can't take your ticket here," said the conductor. "Move on up to the other car."

Ida gave the conductor a polite smile. "The other car is the smoker," she said. "I don't want to sit there."

"Don't matter," the conductor said. "No colored allowed in this car any more. Just move on up to the smoker."

Ida wasn't smiling now. "I'll stay where I am," she said.

"We'll see about that," said the conductor. He reached for Ida's arm. He tried to drag her from her seat. But she grabbed the seat in front of her and held on. "You better behave, darky!" the conductor hissed. He tugged harder on Ida's arm.

Ida's hot temper flared. She sank her teeth into the man's hand. He backed away, his face pale. He left the car.

Ida felt like crying, but she didn't. In the newspapers, she had read about recent changes in the South. After the Civil War, laws had been passed giving black people civil rights. They had the right to be served at restaurants, to sit where they wanted in parks, theatres, and trains. Like white men (but not white women), black men had the right to vote.

But there were still white people who wanted to

take away those rights.   These white people were changing the laws. They were beginning to draw the "color line" all over the South.   Now the "color line" had reached Ida's part of the South.   She wasn't just reading about it in a newspaper.   It was happening *where she was.*

Ida pressed back her tears. "They're not going to put *me* back into slavery!" she thought. "No, nor my people, either." She could see into the smoker as the conductor opened the door.   Black people were crowded in there.   Only Ida had refused to move. "*Somebody's* got to stand up for our rights," Ida thought.

Back came the conductor with two other men. They yanked the slim young woman from her seat. They pushed her roughly down the aisle. Everywhere, white people were standing up, to see. Some of them clapped. Some screamed, "Get her! Show her!"

The train was slowing down. The conductor gave Ida another shove. "You get into the coloreds' place, girl!"

"I will *not!*" Ida said. "Take your hands off me! I am getting off at this station."

The men let go of Ida.   Her hat lay trampled in the aisle. The sleeves of her dress were torn. Her body hurt as she went down the train steps. But she held her head high.

Ida knew what she was going to do. Although some laws had been changed, there were still laws to protect her. Ida went to see a lawyer. He agreed that

Ida could sue the railroad. He said he would be glad to take her case to court.

Meanwhile, Ida went on teaching. When summer came, she began taking classes at Fisk University. This was a black college in Nashville, Tennessee, some miles from Memphis. She also began to study for the examination to teach in Memphis.

Ida enjoyed her life at Fisk and in Memphis. There was much more to do than in Holly Springs. Ida went to hear lectures on many subjects. She went to musical concerts and to plays. Sometimes she saw famous actors perform.

She also went to church picnics and parties. She made some young women friends. Young men came to call on her or to take her for walks. They brought her flowers; some of them wrote her love notes. But none of them interested Ida very much. Friends teased: "Ida has a stone heart!" Ida smiled and said, "Maybe!"

The truth was that Ida had found "my first and only love," as she later called it. That love was journalism. It happened slowly, and it started with her case against the railroad.

In December 1884, Ida won her railroad suit. The white judge, an ex-Union soldier, awarded her damages of five hundred dollars.

Ida was happy. It was not because she had won the money. What mattered to her was that she had won a victory for justice. She wanted black people to know about this victory. She wanted to inspire African-Americans to stand up for their rights.

So Ida wrote the story of her case. She got the story printed in a black church newspaper. The editor of the newspaper was impressed with Ida's writing. He asked her to write a weekly column for the paper. She eagerly said that she would.

Like many writers in those days, Ida used a pen name for her writing. With her first column, Ida became "Iola." People said that Iola's column was "strong medicine." She wrote about injustices to African-Americans. She wrote of special wrongs against black women. She criticized black leaders who failed to speak up for their people. Her column sizzled on the page.

Editors in other parts of the country read Iola's column. They liked her bold, clear style. They wrote and asked Ida to send stories to them. Soon she had articles in black newspapers all over the nation.

While all this was beginning to happen, Ida had some bad news. The railroad had taken its case with Ida to a higher court. In April 1887, the high court reversed the decision. So Ida lost her case, after all.

This was not just bad news for Ida. It was bad news for all African-Americans. One by one, their freedoms were being taken away. Segregation was becoming the law in the South.

But Ida was not going to give up. She knew that if you fight evil, you don't win every time. "But suppose you don't fight?" she thought. "Then there's no chance to win at all."

By this time, Ida had passed the Memphis teachers'

examination. She had a new, better-paid job in the Memphis schools for black children. With money she saved, she become part-owner of a Memphis weekly paper. She also became the editor of this black newspaper, the *Free Speech and Headlight.*

Ida went on working as a teacher. But what she saw in the Memphis schools made her angry and sad. The white school board neglected the black schools. The buildings were run-down and crowded. There were not enough classrooms. Many of the teachers were poorly trained.

Ida needed her teaching job. She earned almost no money from her newspaper work. She knew that she might lose her job if she criticized the schools. So she tried to keep silent.

But after a while, she could not keep silent. She felt that keeping silent made her a partner in the wrongdoing. So she wrote an article about the bad conditions in the black schools. She printed it in the *Free Speech and Headlight.*

When the term ended, the school board did not re-hire Ida for the next year. The board members had heard about Ida's article. They knew that Ida was a good teacher. But, "She's a troublemaker," they told each other. "We don't have to put up with that."

Ida had hoped that some of the black parents would join her protest, but nobody did. That was to happen again and again in the future. Many times Ida battled the causes of black people all alone, before others joined her.

Right now, Ida was out of a job. She wished she could give all her time to newspaper work. She knew now that this was the work she did best. She also knew that it was a good way to serve her race. Black people were ignored in white newspapers—unless they were accused of a crime. Only in the black press could they see themselves as human beings. Only there could they get facts about African-American life.

Ida decided to see if she could make a living with the *Free Speech*. If more people subscribed to the paper, maybe she could.

With that hope, in the summer of 1891, Ida set out to sell subscriptions to the *Free Speech*. She traveled through Tennessee and Mississippi. She went to meetings at black churches and clubs. People were interested in hearing her speak. A woman newspaper reporter was something new. Also, at that time, no other black woman in the country was editing a newspaper.

Many people had read Iola's stories in the black press. It surprised them to see that Ida was so young. (She was twenty-nine and looked younger.) They felt proud of Ida. They admired her fighting spirit. They felt that Ida and the *Free Speech* deserved their support.

It did not cost very much to subscribe to the paper. Hundreds of people signed up and paid the fee. In less than a year, Ida was able to earn a living from the *Free Speech*.

Now Ida could devote herself entirely to journalism. She was happier than she had been since childhood. Her "first and only love" was in her grasp.

CHAPTER 3

Lynch Law

It was late at night. Only one light shone in the offices of the *Free Speech*. The light was over Ida's desk, where she sat reading her mail. She had come back to Memphis that night. She had been away for two weeks, on a business trip.

Ida had not even taken off her hat. She was tired, and looked forward to getting back to Aunt Fannie's house. But she wanted first to see to her mail.

It was a big stack of mail. Letters came from readers in Mississippi, Tennessee, and Arkansas. They thanked Ida for the work she was doing. The *Free Speech* kept up their spirits, by reminding them of their rights.

There were also bills, but Ida wasn't worried about them. The *Free Speech* did not make much money, but it made enough to pay the bills. Ida put the bills to one side, to pay the next day. She picked up another letter and unfolded it.

Suddenly, there was a wild pounding at the door. Ida moved quickly to open it. A man burst in, sweat pouring down his face.

"Miss Wells, Miss Wells!" the man panted. "There's

a white mob down at the People's Grocery! They shot some folks! They're tearing up the store! They're stealing the goods!"

"Why . . . ! Where's Tom?" Ida said. Tom Moss, a mail carrier, was a part-owner of the People's Grocery. His partners, Calvin McDowell and Henry Stewart, worked at the store in the daytime. Tom Moss worked there at night.

"Please calm yourself, Mr. Bowen!" Ida said. "How did this happen? Was Tom at the store?"

"Tom!" Mr. Bowen said. "Oh, my God, Miss Wells— Tom is dead! Calvin and Henry, too! They killed them last night!"

Ida stepped back, her eyes wide with horror. "No," she whispered. Tom Moss and his wife, Betty, were her friends. She was godmother to their little girl.

"Have Tom's wife and child been harmed?" Ida asked.

"Both are safe," said Mr. Bowen. Ida said, "I must go to them. First, I'll go to the People's Grocery. And try to tell me calmly everything that has happened."

Ida got into Mr. Bowen's cart. It was a long way to the People's Grocery. The store was outside the city limits. Most of the people who lived in that area were black.

There had already been a neighborhood grocery before the People's Grocery opened. That store was owned and run by a white man. Then Tom Moss opened his store. After that, most of the black people shopped at Moss's store.

The white store owner was angry about losing his customers. He wanted to shut down the People's Grocery. He looked for ways to get Moss and his partners into trouble. He claimed that the People's Grocery was a place for drinking and gambling. But none of this was true. Moss and his partners were quiet, respect able young men. Everybody knew that.

Finally, while Ida was away, something terrible happened. The white grocer told people that he and his friends were going to "clean out" Moss's store. Moss and his partners asked the police for protection. But the police would not help them.

Then the white gang came. They broke into the People's Grocery with their guns. Friends of Moss and his partners, guarding the store, fired at them. That was all that was needed. Police poured into the store. Moss and his partners were arrested and jailed, along with many other black men.

The next night, a gang of white men was let into the jail. They dragged Tom Moss, Calvin McDowell, and Henry Stewart out of their cells. They took them outside the city limits. There they gouged out their eyes and riddled their bodies with bullets.

Now a bigger white mob had come back to the People's Grocery. They were wrecking and looting the store. Angry black people had gathered on the streets near the store. Some had already been wounded by white gunfire. Ida and Mr. Bowen pleaded with them to go home. So did others who feared a riot and more bloodshed.

Finally, all the black people left. Ida went to Betty Moss. Betty Moss was dry-eyed and brave. From her, Ida learned more facts. This morning, Betty said, a white Memphis paper had printed an eyewitness story of the lynching. This meant that it was known who the murderers were. Therefore, they could be tried and punished for their horrible crimes.

Ida lost no time. She went back to her office and sat down to write. She demanded that the lynchers be brought to justice. "In the name of God and in the name of the law!" she wrote. She printed this demand in the *Free Speech*.

But nothing happened to the lynchers. They were not arrested, tried, or punished. They walked around as free men.

The white newspaper's report on the lynching had quoted Tom Moss's last words. Moss had said, "Tell my people to go West. There is no justice for them here." Now Ida agreed. In mid-March of 1892, she wrote in the *Free Speech*:

> The city of Memphis has made it clear. It will not protect the lives and property of the Negro. It will not allow us to protect ourselves. It will not give us a fair trial in the courts. Instead, it takes us out and murders us in cold blood. There is therefore only one thing left that we can do. Save our money and leave this town.

That was just what the black people of Memphis began to do. Little by little, they began to leave.

Betty Moss, her child, and Tom's parents left soon, for Indiana. Ida was glad they were getting away. But after she had seen them off, she broke down and cried. She cried for them, for Tom, for Calvin, for Henry. In her bedroom at Aunt Fannie's, she wept for the sufferings of all her race.

Then Ida dried her eyes and took up her pen again. In the past six weeks, she had been gathering facts on lynchings. One thing stood out. Almost always it was said that the murdered black men had raped white women. Ida had decided to find out the truth. She had read about hundreds of cases of this kind. She had looked into dozens personally, in Tennessee and Mississippi. In every case, she had found the cry of "rape" untrue.

In most cases, the men who were lynched had not even been charged with rape. Rape was only claimed when a mob came after them. In other cases, white women were the willing partners of black men. When their secret love affairs were discovered, they (or their fathers or brothers) claimed rape. Ida had gathered sworn statements on these cases.

Ida now saw the purpose of lynching. It was to keep black people in a state of fear. It was the white South's way, Ida saw, to "keep the nigger down." The cry of "rape" was only an excuse for lynching. That excuse had not been needed with Tom Moss and his partners. Their "crime" was protecting their property. The lynchers wanted to show that black people had no right to property. They should *stay down*—poor, and humble.

Ida was writing an article about all of this. But she did not have time to finish it that day. She had to pack her bags. She was taking a train that night for Oklahoma. She was going to see what conditions were like there for African-Americans.

More and more black people had been leaving Memphis. The white business people did not like this at all. They needed their black customers. Besides, who would do all the hard, low-paid work black people did?

Many African-Americans were going to Oklahoma. They could get farmland free there. The white business people tried to discourage them. So did the the white newspapers. They printed "scare stories" about Oklahoma. These stories claimed that there wasn't any good land left in Oklahoma. They reported that new settlers were attacked by Indians. They said that storms, hail, and floods in Oklahoma ruined the crops.

So Ida was going to Oklahoma to see for herself. She would send her reports back to the *Free Speech*. Her partner, J.L. Fleming, kept the *Free Speech* going while Ida was away.

Ida traveled in Oklahoma for three weeks. Her firsthand reports were enthusiastic. The farmland was good, and black people were doing well. In Oklahoma, Ida wrote, they had a chance to develop their "manhood and womanhood."

Readers of the *Free Speech* spread the word. In larger numbers than ever, African-Americans set out for Oklahoma. White Memphis business people blamed Ida—and they were correct. Ida's readers trusted her. They did not trust white Memphis.

Ida thought that Oklahoma might be a good place for her to settle, too. She wrote to Aunt Fannie about it. She wrote and asked Mr. Fleming to think about moving the *Free Speech*. "Let's talk it over when I return," Ida wrote. "I am going to New York next week, to cover the church conference. I will see what our prospects may be in New York, too."

Just before Ida left for New York, she finished her article on lynching. She sent it to the *Free Speech* from Oklahoma City.

In New York, Ida was met by Mr. Thomas T. Fortune. He was the editor of an important black newspaper, the *New York Age*. He was a great admirer of Ida, who often wrote pieces for the *Age*.

Mr. Fortune said, "We've been a long time getting you to New York. But now you're here, I guess you'll have to stay."

Ida smiled. "Not without the *Free Speech*," she said.

"Why, Miss Wells," said Mr. Fortune, "Haven't you seen the morning paper?"

Something in his voice made Ida feel afraid. The smile faded from her face. "No."

"My dear Miss Wells," said Mr. Fortune. "There is no more *Free Speech*. A white mob has destroyed it. Your last article on lynching was too much for Memphis! All the trains are being watched for you. If you go home, they will kill you on sight."

CHAPTER 4

A Crusade Begins

Ida's first thought was for the safety of her *Free Speech* partner. "What has happened to Mr. Fleming?" she cried.

Thomas T. Fortune gently led the dazed Ida through the crowded train station. He said: "Your partner sent me a telegram. He asked me to tell you that he got out of Memphis safely. He won't return— and he begs you not to."

"But—"

"I think he's right, Miss Wells. He says that some colored men have formed a group to protect you. You know what that means if you go back? It means more bloodshed! More useless deaths!"

Ida said sadly, "I know. The only useful weapon we have now is telling the truth. But the *Free Speech* was my weapon for truth. And it's gone!"

"You can still tell the truth. You still have your *pen*. Come to work for the *New York Age*!" said Mr. Fortune.

Ida hesitated. She was still in a state of shock. She was thinking: "The *Free Speech*—gone!"

Mr. Fortune said, "You have done a brave job with

the *Free Speech*, Miss Wells. But please think. Your paper only got to people in a few Southern states. The *New York Age* is a big paper. It's read by people all over the country. Think of the thousands you might reach with your words!"

Ida's spirits lifted a little. They went out into the noisy streets of New York. "Think about it a while, Miss Wells," said Mr. Fortune. "But now, we're going to my house. Mrs. Fortune has a fine dinner planned for you!" He whistled for a cab.

A week later, Ida went to work at the *Age*. Aunt Fannie had sent word that she, too, was leaving Memphis. She was taking Ida's two youngest sisters to California. Now nothing was left for Ida in Memphis—except threats against her life. The mob that destroyed the *Free Speech* had warned, in a note left at the scene, that death awaited her if she returned. The leading white Memphis newspaper had called for her to be "tied to a stake and burned."

Ida's life had been in danger from the first time she wrote to protest the lynching of Tom Moss and his partners. She had known that, but it hadn't stopped her from writing about lynching. She wasn't going to stop now that she was safe in the North. In the pages of the *Age*, she could publish all the facts she had gathered. She could tell the whole story about so-called black rapists and their white lynchers.

Part of that story was about the rape of *black* women by *white* men. It had started in slavery times, and still went on. White men forced sex on black women any time they wanted to. There was nobody to protect the women. Black people did not have the power to protect them. And the whites who had power would not protect them. They saw no harm in the raping of black women by white men.

But suppose a black man was accused of raping a white woman? Without any trial, he was tortured and murdered. And who were his killers? The same whites whose men raped black women!

There was no way to know the number of black women raped by white men. Rape was a secret act. But most lynchings were public. They were mob events. And every year there were more of them. Ida knew this from the figures she had gathered.

She also knew that people were starting to believe the excuse the lynchers gave. People were beginning to think that black men were a threat to white women. If a lie is told often enough, people come to believe it.

It was not only enemies of black people who believed the lie. Friendly whites, who might have spoken up against the lynchings, were silent. They didn't want to defend men who might be rapists. Most black people were silent, too.

"We can't stop the lynchings if we don't stop the lies!" Ida said. That was why it was so important for her to get her story to the public. And through the *Age*, she did that.

The *Age* printed her story on the front page. There was a huge headline. The story was seven columns long. It gave names, places, and dates of the lynchings.

It gave proof of the innocence of the men who had been lynched. The *Age* printed ten thousand copies and sent them throughout the country.

Ida hoped that white newspapers would pick up her story. The white press often reported on stories printed by the *New York Age*. But the white press kept silence on Ida's story.

Ida was bitterly disappointed. If lynching was to be stopped, white people, as well as black, would have to help.

Before a year passed, white people *were* helping. But it was not because of the white newspapers. It was because of the efforts of black women in New York. At first, there were only two women. They discussed Ida's article during a visit with each other. Then they invited some other friends to talk about it. The group of women quickly grew to two hundred and fifty.

These women were grateful to Ida for giving the real facts of lynching. They knew that Ida had been run out of Memphis for her courage. They knew it took courage, too, for her to write about rape—even in New York. In the 1890s, rape was not openly talked about, much less written about. The women wanted to do something to honor Ida's bravery. They also wanted to raise money to help her crusade against lynching.

On October 5, 1892, these women held a great meeting at Lyric Hall, in New York. Above the platform, "Iola," Ida's pen name, was spelled out in electric lights. The hall was jammed with women. Black women leaders from New York, Brooklyn, Philadelphia, and Boston were there.

At the meeting, the women raised five hundred dollars for the crusade. They gave Ida a gold brooch in the shape of a pen. (Ever after, she wore it for all important events.) Many women gave outstanding speeches, but Ida's speech was the best.

Ida had been nervous about her speech. She had spoken in public before, but mostly she was a writer. Besides, she had never given a speech about lynching. It was painful to talk about people being shot, burned, hanged. It was terrible to speak about the mobs cheering their deaths. Yet in a clear voice, Ida told it all.

That night was the beginning of the black women's club movement. It is a movement that continues to the present day. Black women's clubs still work in countless ways to make a better world. The New York women who had planned the Lyric Hall meeting decided to go on working. They formed a club called the Women's Loyal Union. Their first work was setting up speaking dates for Ida in other cities. Women in other cities formed clubs to help.

One of the cities where Ida spoke before black women was Boston. It was there that she was first invited to speak to a white group. It was a group of suffragists, people working for women's right to vote. Next, a white minister asked Ida to speak at his church.

A white Boston newspaper reported on Ida's talks to these groups. At last, Ida's story had reached some white readers.

Then Ida's story began to reach *outside* the United States. She had used her gift of five hundred dollars to print a booklet on lynching. It was a longer version of her *Age* article, titled *Southern Horrors.* A visiting Englishwoman read the booklet. She took it home. In Scotland, she gave it to a friend.

The woman's friend decided to help Ida's anti-lynching crusade. She gathered others who wanted to help. They asked Ida to come to Great Britain to speak. They said they would pay her expenses. Ida at once said yes.

In 1893, people traveled much less than they do today. Visiting a foreign country was rare, except for people with money. And except for a few daring spirits, single women did not travel alone. It was an unusual event when Ida Wells, an African-American woman just out of the South, boarded her ship.

Ida was *very* seasick on the ship to England. But after she landed, she felt fine. Everywhere she spoke, in England and Scotland, great crowds came to hear her. The newspapers were full of her story. It was not like the United States, where her words dashed against a wall of white silence.

That was why Ida had come. She knew that Americans wanted the British to have a good opinion of them. They wanted the British to believe that the United States was "the land of the free." When Ida told about the way black Americans were treated, Great Britain was shocked. A wave of protest began to rise across the land. It included threats that British people would stop buying U.S. goods. White Americans paid attention to *that*.

In *Southern Horrors*, Ida had written:

> The appeal to the white man's pocket has always been more effectual than appeals made to his conscience. The white man's dollar is his god. Stop his dollar and many outrages against Afro-Americans will stop.

The facts that Ida laid before the British public were reported in many white newspapers across the U.S. The silence had been broken.

After a two-month tour, Ida sailed for home. She had gotten what she came for. As her ship headed back across the ocean, she didn't feel the least bit seasick.

CHAPTER 5

Not the "Only Love"

"Ida! How glad I am that you are here!"

The man holding Ida's hands in a warm grasp was tall and stately. His halo of white hair, his white beard, gleamed against his bronze skin. His fine eyes were piercing but gentle. He was Frederick Douglass, the great African-American leader.

With a spring breeze blowing the ribbons of her hat, Ida walked alongside tall Mr. Douglass. They were on the grounds of the 1893 World's Fair, in Chicago. Sparkling stone buildings lined the walks. Fountains sent up lacy sprays of water. Tall columns holding giant statues reached into the air.

People turned to gaze at the majestic-looking Mr. Douglass. His fame had made his face well known to many. His picture was often in the newspapers. After his own escape from slavery, he had become a leader in the anti-slavery movement. He was also among the first few men who had joined women in their drive for equal rights. He had held a number of high positions, most recently as U.S. Minister to Haiti.

A year ago, Mr. Douglass had read Ida's *Age* piece on lynching. He had been moved and impressed. He had traveled from his home in Washington, D.C., just to meet Ida. After that, Ida had become friends with him, his wife, and children.

Now Ida was in Chicago because Mr. Douglass had asked her to come. He had said: "We need your help at the World's Fair."

Chicago's Fair was called the World's Columbian Exposition. Begun in October 1892, the Fair marked four hundred years since Columbus had landed in America. Nations from all over the world had exhibits at the Fair. So did almost every ethnic group in the U.S., including Asians, Hispanics, and Native Americans. But one group was missing. African-Americans had not been invited. The requests of their leaders for exhibit space had been turned down.

"We must make this outrage known!" Frederick Douglass said. Before Ida left for England, he told her his plan. "What we need, Ida, is a book about Afro-Americans, to give visitors to the Fair. It must be a book that tells how our race has been held down. It must tell of the progress we have made in spite of that. It must tell of all we have done for this country!"

Ida was already at work on the book. It was to contain articles by a number of black American writers. Ida's first task had been getting in touch with these writers. From England, she had sent letters to each one, asking for an article.

One of the people to whom Ida had sent a letter was Ferdinand Lee Barnett. He was the publisher of a weekly paper, the *Chicago Conservator*. He was also a lawyer. Ida had not yet met him. Mr. Douglass had a very high opinion of him, she knew.

Mr. Douglass said now, "Ferdinand Barnett has his article ready for you. He wants to give it to you in person. He's coming down to meet us in an hour, at the Haiti building."

At the Haiti building, many people were waiting to see Mr. Douglass. He was in charge of the exhibit from the small black republic of Haiti. Since black Americans had no exhibit of their own, black visitors often met at the Haiti building. It seemed every one of them wanted to shake Mr. Douglass's hand! Visitors from many foreign lands also wanted to see or speak to him.

Mr. Douglass barely had time to show Ida to a little desk in the lobby. "This is your work space," he said. "It's noisy, but you're used to noisy newspaper offices." A crowd of people wafted him away. He called back: "I'll send Mr. Barnett to you."

Half an hour later, Ida was writing down some notes about the Fair. A voice above her head said, "Miss Wells?"

Ida looked up. The man standing before her was tall and slender, in a well-cut suit. His wavy hair was just touched with gray, and he wore a trim moustache. He was very handsome.

"I'm Ferdinand Lee Barnett," he said. "I've really been looking forward to meeting you. I've been following 'Iola's' career for a number of years. Oh—" He placed a neat stack of papers on her desk. "I've brought my article. I thought if I brought it in person,

I could ask you to lunch with me."

"You're the first one to give me an article for the Fair book," Ida said. "You're very prompt. And *I* am very hungry!"

Barnett laughed. "Perfect combination," he said.

Ida and Barnett seemed to be a "perfect combination" in many ways. In the weeks that followed, they saw a lot of each other. They had many interests in common. Both were active in the struggle for African-American rights. Both were journalists. They shared a love for books, music, and the theatre.

Yet they were different from each other, too. Ida was a fiery, intense person. She was always stirred up. Barnett knew how to relax. He could sit back, look at himself and the world, and laugh. He made Ida laugh, too.

"I'm good for you, Ida," Ferdinand said one afternoon, about six weeks after their first meeting. "You've only lost your temper three times this week. I'm very good for your character. I think you'd better marry me."

It was not the first time Ferdinand had asked Ida to marry him. He had proposed to her daily for two weeks, by letter and in person. And Ida, by now, knew that journalism was no longer her "only love." But it was still her first love. She said, "I care about you, yes. But my work comes first. I can't give it up!"

"I wouldn't want you to." Ferdinand looked serious now. "Your work for our people is too important to me."

Ida said, "I just don't have time to get married."

"Doesn't take much time," said Ferdinand. "About fifteen minutes. That is, unless you want a fancy wedding."

"*I* don't want a wedding at *all*," answered Ida.

They continued to joke in this way about marriage, through the hot summer months. Meanwhile, Ida's work on the Fair booklet went forward. All the writers had now sent their articles to her. Mr. Douglass's, the most important one, was nearly complete. He and Ida had decided on a title for the book. It would be called *The Reason Why the Colored American Is Not in the World's Columbian Exposition.*

But there was a problem. It would cost more than five hundred dollars to print the book. Mr. Douglass had so far been unable to raise the money. "I'd counted on more help from our people," he told Ida. "We must depend on them, above all."

Ida said, "I think I know some people of our race who will help out. Let me try it, anyway."

So Ida turned to women. And, as before, black women came to her rescue. They helped—and they did it quickly.

The women arranged a series of public meetings at various black churches. They advertised the meetings through the churches. They also put up many posters to announce that Frederick Douglass and Ida B. Wells would speak.

The black people of Chicago wanted to see and hear the great Frederick Douglass. They were very interested in hearing "Iola" speak, too. The church meetings were crowded. At the end of each meeting, people donated money for the booklet. There was soon enough money to have twenty thousand copies printed.

Ida was at her desk at the Haiti building every day, giving out copies of *The Reason Why.* Thousands of fair visitors read the book. They learned many things they hadn't known about the achievements of black Americans. They also learned about white America— how it robbed black people of education, jobs, even the right to vote. When the visitors left, they took the book home with them. It traveled far—to Peru, Germany, France, Russia, India.

Ida was getting ready to travel far, too, after the Fair ended. She had been invited to return to Great Britain, this time for a longer visit. She would be gone six months.

Before she left Chicago, Ida went to the offices of a paper called the *Inter-Ocean.* The Chicago *Inter-Ocean* had taken a strong stand against lynching. It was the only white daily paper in the U.S. to do so. Ida went to thank the editor.

The editor was glad to see Ida. He had read her articles and thought she was an outstanding reporter. He invited her to send letters to his paper, reporting on her trip. He said the paper would pay for her reports. Very surprised, Ida said yes.

So Ida became the first black foreign correspondent for a white American paper. Even today—with TV and radio, besides newspapers—a black U.S. foreign corre-spondent is rare. A black *woman* in this job is even more rare.

While still in Chicago, Ida helped start the city's first black women's club. (After Ida was in Britain, the women named it the Ida B. Wells Club.) This club be-came an important force for bettering the lives of black Chicagoans and other Americans.

Ida did something important in her private life, too. She told Ferdinand that she would marry him. She wouldn't say *when*. But she said that when she came back, she would move from New York to Chi-cago. She had already written Mr. Fortune that she was not returning to *The Age*.

For the moment, Ferdinand had to be content with that.

CHAPTER 6

Private Life and Public Duty

Ida began her second visit to Great Britain in the winter of 1894. In the months since her first visit, the British anti-lynching crusade had died down. It needed to be fired up again. The letter asking Ida to visit said, "We need your help."

And Ida needed British help. Lynching *had spread* in the U.S.—even beyond the South. There had been lynchings in Illinois, Indiana, Iowa, Ohio, and Pennsylvania. Nothing had been done to punish the killers. The crimes had been hushed up.

"Why have I traveled thousands of miles to speak to you?" said Ida. She was speaking in a crowded London church. "Because my race cannot get a hearing in its own country! The white press and the white pulpit are closed to us! We must depend upon the English press and pulpit to speak out for justice!"

Ida's big dark eyes flashed. Her face glowed. Her voice rang. Over the past year, she had become a powerful speaker.

"Black men, women—even *children*—have been lynched by white mobs in America. Nearly 2,000 souls died this way in the past ten years. No one knows if any of them was guilty of any crime. They were never tried in any court!

"You have looked into the facts and looked into your hearts. When Americans do the same, the law will protect Negro and white alike. Help us to end our country's shame!"

The audience rose. The clapping was long and loud.

Ida's message spread across Britain. She was invited to meet with members of the government and the nobility. She met with leading clergymen. She was the guest of editors of leading newspapers. All promised to use their influence in the United States to stop mob law.

In every city Ida visited, she helped to form an anti-lynching group. Each group was headed by an important person. (A son-in-law of Queen Victoria was the head of one group.) These groups would carry on the crusade after Ida left.

When Ida sailed for home, she carried an important letter. It was an appeal from ministers of every Christian faith in Great Britain. It asked white Christian ministers in the United States to allow Ida to speak in their churches.

It was hard for the white ministers to turn down this request. Their British Christian brothers wrote that they were sure Ida B. Wells spoke the truth. "Suppose she really *is* telling the truth?" the white ministers thought. "*Are* innocent people being butchered?"

None of the ministers to whom Ida showed the letter turned her down. Little by little, they began to believe the facts Ida gave in her speeches. These ministers now wrote statements against lynching. Other ministers signed them. Churches that had been against slavery joined the anti-lynching cause.

Many other groups besides churches invited Ida to lecture when she returned. The groups were everywhere except the South—from Maine to California. It would take at least a year to travel to them all.

"A *year?*" Ferdinand said. "Well. Let's say a year, then. You know that I would wait for you forever, Ida. But please . . . not more than a year!"

Ida was away lecturing until a week before her marriage. She had no time to plan the wedding. But she didn't need to. The Ida B. Wells Club took care of everything. Its members reserved the church. They sent invitations to the guests Ida and Ferdinand wanted. They saw to the flowers and the cake.

Ida's two youngest sisters came to the wedding from California. They were grown young women now. Although Ida never earned much money, she had helped to put them through college. Now she wanted them for her bridesmaids. She also found time to have a bridal gown made, of satin and lace. So the wedding turned out to be a fancy one, after all.

Ida was not quite thirty-three. She was no longer a skinny, pretty little girl. She was a poised, lovely woman. Her proud walk made her look taller than she was. In her white satin gown with its long train, she looked queenly.

Moving down the aisle toward Ferdinand, Ida smiled to herself. She was thinking of the words of her Memphis friends, years ago. "Ida has a stone heart!" Her heart, when she looked at Ferdinand—or even thought of him—was anything but stone.

Both Ida and Ferdinand had many friends. Through their work for racial equality, they each knew hundreds of people. There was a big crowd of guests at their wedding party.

Not long after their marriage, Ida and Ferdinand both began new jobs. Ferdinand became assistant state's attorney for the county. He was the first African-American to hold that position. And Ida, before she married Ferdinand, had bought the *Conservator* from him and his partners. She took charge of it the Monday after the wedding.

Ida was busier than ever. But she was not too busy to get pregnant. Within a year of marrying, she gave birth to a son.

Ferdinand, who was a widower, already had two sons. His mother ran the house and took care of his boys. Ida enjoyed his little boys, but she didn't long for babies of her own. She had already reared babies— her own sisters and brothers.

Ida knew about the birth control methods of her day. Why did she choose motherhood? No one knows, for she never told anyone. She and Ferdinand had three more children over the next few years.

Four children didn't slow Ida down much. In part,

that was because of Ferdinand. He didn't *want* Ida slowed down. When he had said, "Your work is important to me," he meant it. What's more, he did something about it.

Four months after the first baby was born, Ida was asked to go to an important meeting. From all the black women's clubs in the nation, women were meeting in Washington, D.C. They were to decide on ways to work together to make their work stronger. The women of the Ida B. Wells Club wanted Ida to represent them.

Ida was still breast-feeding her infant, Charles. "I won't be able to go," she said sadly. "I can't leave Charles."

"You can take Charles." Ferdinand said. "He'd love it."

"Well, *I* wouldn't love it. I'd have to spend all my time taking care of him! So what's the use of going?"

Ferdinand took a deep breath. "Now, Ida, don't lose your temper. I'm hiring a nurse to take care of Charles on the trip."

Ida didn't lose her temper. She was delighted. "What a wonderful idea!" she said. "Why didn't I think of it myself?"

"Because you don't have my *brains*," Ferdinand said.

Ida threw a pillow at his head. Then she began to get ready for the trip.

Two months after the Washington, D.C., meetings, Charles went traveling again. This time, Ida gave speeches in towns all over the state of Illinois. Her speaking tour was set up by the Republican women of the state.

Like most African-Americans of her time, Ida was still a loyal Republican. President Lincoln, "the Great Emancipator," had been a Republican. Also, once in a while, the Republican Party spoke up for black people's rights. So Ida went around the state giving dozens of speeches to white Republican women.

Women with nursing babies didn't go around making public speeches in 1896. But Ida did it, and Ferdinand backed her up.

Still, sometimes Ida wasn't sure she was doing the right thing. Maybe she should be giving more time to her baby, she thought. The next year, she had another baby, Herman. That was when Ida decided it was time to retire.

She sold *The Conservator.* She gave up her speaking tours. She stayed at home with the babies and Ferdinand's boys. She found that she enjoyed this. She felt happy and content.

But for Ida B. Wells, a quiet home life was not to be. Her quiet life lasted only five months, until February 1898.

It was then that a brutal lynching took place in South Carolina. A black man, Frazier Baker, had been named postmaster for his town. Some whites didn't like that. A few days after Baker took his new job, a mob went to his home. There were more than three hundred white men. They set fire to the Baker house.

As the Baker family tried to escape, the white men fired on them. They badly wounded Mrs. Baker and four of the Baker children. They shot Mr. Baker and the fifth child to death. The bodies burned where they fell in the house.

These events shook Ida deeply. Her grief moved her into action. As a postmaster, Ida thought, Mr. Baker had held a federal job. This meant the U.S. government could—and should—punish his killers. "The *President* must act," Ida thought.

Ida led a group of citizens from Illinois to see President William McKinley. She demanded, among other things, that the President ask Congress to outlaw lynching. "Is this country," Ida asked him, "with its power to defend its citizens abroad, unable to protect them at home? We refuse to believe it!"

McKinley listened respectfully. He promised to do "all in my power." So did the members of Congress Ida went to see. But in spite of Ida's pleas, little was done.

After a month in the nation's capital, Ida headed home. She felt sick at heart. Yet this failure did not make Ida decide it was best to stay at home. It had a different effect.

Yes, Ida thought, it was important to take care of your children. But surely, she thought, it was just as important to carry on the fight for justice!

From now on, she would try to do both.

Quarrels Among Friends

The train whistle blew. Ida blew a last kiss to Ferdinand through the window. Holding Herman in his arms, Ferdinand waved the baby's small hand. Ferdinand's sons, Albert and Ferdinand, Jr., waved and shouted. Little Charles jumped up and down.

The train lurched. Then it moved forward slowly, and then faster. Ida's family glided from sight.

It was not a year since Ida's visit to President McKinley. Now, in 1898, she was heading east again. This time she was going to Rochester, New York.

It was autumn, growing cold. Ida wore a warm wool suit in a dark, rich shade of green. She opened a book but did not read. She gazed out at the trees, still touched with red and gold.

Ida did not see the trees. She was remembering another train journey. It was fifteen years since she'd been thrown off that train from Memphis. The South had just begun making laws to separate blacks and whites then. Now these Jim Crow laws ruled the South. There was no way for black people to get ahead there. They were lucky if they just stayed alive.

Yet, as Ida gazed through the train window, she felt

hopeful. If she hadn't felt hope, she would not have been on the train. She would be at home. Maybe she would be reading a story to the boys, or enjoying a joke with Ferdinand, or baking pies with his mother. Instead, she was speeding to a meeting.

It was this meeting that gave Ida hope. It was to be a big meeting of African-Americans. Men and women leaders from North and South were coming together. They were going to combine their strength. They were going to unite in one big organization.

Ida had long dreamed of such an organization. If they all worked together, Ida thought, they *could* make this country change.

Now Ida noticed the trees beyond the train window. She watched their leaves drift down. Dusk fell. Inside the train, the lamps went on. Ida could see no more in the dark outside.

She opened her book and began to read.

"I just don't understand you—not at all!" Ida was having an argument with her old friend Mr. Fortune, editor of the *New York Age*. They were talking in a hallway during a break in the meeting.

Ida was having arguments with a lot of old friends. Other people were arguing, too. They had been meeting for two days. So far, about the only thing they'd agreed on was a name for the new organization. It would be called the Afro-American Council.

But they could not agree on what kind of policy to follow. Some people, like Ida, wanted to take strong stands. They wanted a statement against President McKinley, who had done nothing about mob killings. They wanted to fight Jim Crow laws. But others were against these kinds of actions. "We have to go slow," they said.

"Slow?" Ida snapped. "You mean *backward!*"

Ida put a hand to her forehead. She felt so tired of arguing with the leading people of her race! "If only Frederick Douglass were still with us!" she thought.

But Mr. Douglass had died three years earlier. Since then, there was a new African-American leader. The "go slow" people were his followers. His name was Booker T. Washington. He was head of Tuskegee Institute, an important black school in Alabama. He thought that black people should accept the Jim Crow system. He wanted them to be honest, hardworking— and quiet.

Ida didn't believe in being quiet. She knew that African-Americans were tired of struggling. She knew they felt that fighting for their rights had not brought many results. But it had brought *some,* Ida thought. For example, the number of lynchings was slowly but surely going down. "That didn't happen because we were *quiet!*" Ida said to Mr. Fortune.

"Your newspaper helped me start the anti-lynching movement," Ida said. "You've fought so hard against the wrongs to our race. Don't you believe the Afro-American Council can do the same?"

Mr. Fortune shook his head. "There's a time and a place for everything," he said.

Ida's eyes blazed. "Yes!" she said. "The time is *now*. The place is *here*. It always *is!*"

She turned from him and marched back to the meeting. There she gave a passionate speech. Her speech won many people at the meeting to her viewpoint. Still, when the meeting ended, the "go slow" people had won many of their points. The policy chosen by the Afro-American Council was not what Ida had hoped for.

Mr. Fortune wasn't a "go slow" person. However, he didn't think the time was ripe for a strong black organization. He was more right in his judgment than Ida was. The Afro-American Council was not the strong, united group she had dreamed of.

But for now, Ida thought, it would have to do.

"Come in. Come *in* out of this dreadful rain. Oh, my dear, how tired you look! Now tell me all that has happened. I'm so sorry I missed the council meeting! I felt I had to be at my suffrage meeting in New York. There just wasn't time to get back here to Rochester— Let me take your coat. You're *dripping!*"

The woman who led Ida to a chair near the fireplace was over seventy. Her white hair was drawn tightly over her ears into a bun. Very thin, taller than Ida, she wore a plain black dress. Next to Ida, blooming and pretty, her hair shining with rain, the woman looked stern. But her gray eyes glowed warmly at Ida.

"China tea!" Ida said. She took a sip from her cup. "Oh, this feels good! Oh, how glad I am to be here!"

The woman who sat near Ida at the fireplace was a white person. Ida did not trust a lot of white people. But this woman she trusted, admired, and loved. The woman was Susan B. Anthony. She was one of the great leaders of the women's suffrage movement. She was also an important friend to African-American rights. Long before Ida's birth, Miss Anthony had worked in the anti-slavery cause. She went on working now for racial equality.

"Did Mr. Washington show his face today? Tell me everything that happened!" Miss Anthony repeated.

Ida told Miss Anthony about the quarrels at the meeting. "Mr. Washington wasn't there. But his followers won a lot," she ended by saying. "Now—tell me about the suffrage meeting."

"Quarrels there, too—as usual!" Miss Anthony said. "But also some progress. It's slow. But one day we *will* win the vote for women. And then—everything will change!"

Ida frowned. "You often say so, Miss Anthony. I can't agree. Women ought to have the right to vote, surely! But I don't think that will change the world much. For example—women aren't any better than men on the color question."

Miss Anthony didn't answer. She thought Ida had quarreled enough today. "You're tired," she said. "And I'm tiring you more. It's time for bed for you. Your room's all ready."

But the next day there was a quarrel.

Ida had known Miss Anthony before she'd married

Ferdinand Barnett. Since then, she noticed that Miss Anthony sometimes said "*Mrs.* Barnett!" in a biting voice. Ida noticed it at breakfast today, more than once.

At last, Ida said: "The way you call me *Mrs.*! Don't you believe in women getting married, Miss Anthony?"

Miss Anthony put down her cup. "Yes," she said. "But not women leaders as important as you! I too might have married. But it would have meant dropping my work."

Her gray eyes rested on Ida in dismay. "You're the best person in this country at your work! But these days, your mind is often not *on* your work. It's because you have a divided duty. Here you are in Rochester because you think the Afro-American Council needs you. But you also feel your babies need you at home. Now, isn't that true?"

"No, it isn't!" Ida said hotly. "My children are in very good hands with their grandmother and their father!"

"Yes," Miss Anthony said. "But I suspect you think they ought to be *your* hands. In your place, I know I would."

Ida was silent. She was angry because what Miss Anthony had said was true. She felt torn between duty to her children and duty to her race. Miss Anthony had made her choices long ago. But Ida was still in the midst of her choices.

Now Miss Anthony said, "Forgive me for being sharp with you, my dear. A finer, braver woman than you never lived! Whatever you do, I'm proud to be your friend."

The two friends parted on good terms. It was not their first quarrel—nor their last. Both were strong-willed women. Yet they remained friends to the end of Miss Anthony's life.

Heading home to Chicago on the train, Ida thought of her "divided duty." She didn't know what to do about it. Her race needed her, she thought—and so did her children. She felt that as the children grew older they would need her still more.

Two years later, Ida and Ferdinand had another child, a girl. They named her "Ida B. Wells, Jr." People named boys "junior" for their fathers, Ida and Ferdinand said. "So why not name a girl 'junior' for her mother!" In 1904, another girl was born to them. She was their last child, named Alfreda.

Ida traveled less now. With Ferdinand, she took a hand in her children's education. With him, she saw to it that they did their homework. She went visiting at their schools; she talked with their teachers. She took them to church. She liked to dress them up for Halloween and plan their birthday parties.

Ida did the best she could with her "divided duty." She gave her children time, love, care. But she also went on writing, speaking, working for justice. As the twentieth century began, Ida B. Wells was "trying to do both."

CHAPTER 8

In the Windy City

While her children were small, Ida did not travel far from Chicago. But in Chicago, often called "the Windy City," Ida's life was full. She had more to do than hours for doing it.

She went on with her fight against lynching. But that was only part of what she did. More and more, Ida turned her attention to Chicago. She wanted to make it a better city for black Americans.

Many of Chicago's black people were poor. Few earned wages equal to white wage-earners. African-Americans were not treated with the same respect as whites. Still, unlike in the South, black inequality was not written down *in law*.

In Chicago, in 1900, the two races were not yet badly divided. Although there was a ghetto where many black people lived, others lived in the same neighborhoods as whites. Whites and blacks shared the same parks. Their children went to the same schools. All these things made Ida feel some hope for the Windy City.

But one morning Ida woke up to read an upsetting story in the *Chicago Tribune*. The *Tribune* was the leading white newspaper in the city. The story argued that blacks and whites would be better off in separate schools. The next day, there was another story of the same kind. Another followed, the day after.

Ida knew about separate schools. She had taught in such schools, in the South. She knew the black schools were always the ones cheated of money. She had lost her teaching job for telling the truth about this.

Now Ida sat down and wrote a letter to the *Tribune.* It was a powerful letter that argued against separate schools.

Ida had written many letters to the *Tribune* in the past. The paper had almost always printed the letters. But this time, a week went by, and then another. The letter was not printed.

Ida went to see the editor of the *Tribune.* "You have not printed my letter," Ida told him. "You have not printed a word from *any* Negro on the school question."

The editor said: "Yours is the only letter of protest I have seen. I don't think other colored people share your views."

"I'm sure that's not true," said Ida. "And I'll be glad to prove it. May I bring some others of my race to talk with you?"

"I don't have time for that," the editor said. He looked at his watch. "Perhaps I may print a part of your letter. I can't say when, though." He stood up. "I am very busy, Mrs. Barnett."

"Yes, I see that," Ida said. "Good day to you!"

She swept out of his office, her head held high. To herself, she thought: "You're going to be busier than you think!"

That very day Ida telephoned her friend Jane Addams. Miss Addams was perhaps the best-known woman in America at that time. She was famous as a reformer. She was the founder of Chicago's Hull House. This was a place set up to help poor people, especially through education.

Ida told Miss Addams her story. "The opinions of my race mean nothing to the *Tribune*," said Ida. "But I'm sure there are white people who don't want separate schools. Could you call together some people of influence who would help us?"

Miss Addams at once said yes. The following Sunday there was a meeting at Hull House. There were judges, ministers, a rabbi—all of them well-known in Chicago. There was even a member of the board of education.

All agreed with Ida about separate schools. "The people of Chicago don't want separate schools! We'll go see the *Tribune* editor about this," they said. And they did.

Ida did not know what they said to the editor. But the *Tribune* printed no more arguments for separate schools.

Ferdinand said to Ida: "What a good idea it was, to take the problem to Miss Addams! Why didn't I think of it?"

"You just don't have my *brains*," Ida said. And she

reached up and kissed him on the chin.

Soon after these events, Ida and Ferdinand bought a big house. Their family was growing. Though Ida didn't have nurses now, she always had someone to do housework. Sometimes the women she hired wanted a room as well as a job. Also, Ferdinand and Ida often had out-of-town guests. They needed a lot of room.

When they moved into their new neighborhood, in 1901, they were the only non-white family. But over the next years, more black people moved into the area. There began to be trouble.

One day Charles came home with a bloody nose. He had been attacked by some white boys. A gang of them began to follow Charles and Herman home from school. When some older black boys formed a gang to protect the children, the attacks died down.

But Ida felt bitter. To Ferdinand, she said: "Mr. Washington says all we have to do is work hard, and be good. He thinks that's how to prevent a race war. What he won't face is we're already *in* a race war. Not just in the South. Here, too!"

Ferdinand shook his head. "Oh, *Ida!*" he said.

"Don't you 'oh-Ida' *me*, Ferdinand Lee Barnett!" cried Ida.

Then she sighed. "I'm sorry."

Ferdinand went to Ida and put his arms around her. "One thing for sure, Ida," he said. "Marrying me didn't do a darn thing for your temper!"

Ida's temper didn't improve much during the next

few years. She saw conditions for black people in Chicago grow worse. Thousands of them were moving into the city from the South. They couldn't make a living in the South, and their lives were always in danger there. They moved North to find a better life.

They did not find a better life in Chicago. The women got along a little better than the men. They, at least, could find housecleaning jobs. But most of the men could not find steady work. Many of them stopped trying. Some turned to crime.

Ida could not sit by and watch this happen. As always, she knew she had to "do something." She set to work on the problem. She roused other people to help, too.

This time, she turned to some young men in her church. Under her leadership, they started a storefront center. They called it the Negro Fellowship League Reading Room and Social Center. It was in the most rough-and-tough part of the black ghetto. The street was lined with saloons and gambling joints. That was where the down-and-out men hung around.

It wasn't long before these men started coming to the center. They could rest and talk there, read newspapers, play games, sing around the piano. For fifteen cents, they could have a clean bed. A friend of Ida's owned a nearby cafe. He gave meals to the men for a special, low price. Most important, the center helped the men find jobs.

There was no other place where these men could find help in Chicago. In 1910, when the center started, even the YMCA did nothing for black men. Some rich white people thought that was wrong. They heard Ida speak at a white church about plans for the center. They gave Ida money to help start the center.

Later, Ida took a job and gave her salary to the center. Her job was as a court probation officer. That was useful, too. She was able to help men at the center who were on parole. And Ferdinand donated many hours to legal work for their court cases.

Black people with money didn't give the center as much help as Ida thought they should. The black church members who helped displeased her at times, too. Some of them were afraid of the center's rough neighborhood, or distrusted the poor blacks who lived there. Ida thought that these people were selfish and hard-hearted. She was often unhappy with what she called "the race's so-called better class."

She was also unhappy with black women who showed no interest in women's suffrage. True, she sometimes argued on this subject with her suffrage leader friend Susan B. Anthony. But Ida, too, was eager for women to have the vote. She was especially eager for black women to be able to vote. She thought that African-Americans could use voting to increase their power.

Ida had worked with white women's suffrage groups for years. At last, on a snowy day in January 1913, she founded a black group. It was called the Alpha Suffrage Club. It was the first black women's suffrage group in the nation.

That same year, a new President, Woodrow Wilson, was about to take office. The women's suffrage groups wanted him to help their cause. To get his attention, they marched in the streets. In Chicago, the women held a huge parade. The women of the Alpha Suffrage Club marched alongside their white suffrage sisters.

All the women in the parade wore white dresses with purple sashes. Among them were Ida and Alfreda, now nine. Holding her mother's hand, Alfreda felt very proud.

A few months later, women from all over the country went to Washington, D.C., to demand the vote. Ida was among the women from Illinois who went to the parade. But trouble arose.

The leaders of the parade asked Ida not to march. There were white women from the South in the parade. These women said they wouldn't march in the same parade with Ida.

But the women from Illinois knew Ida had a right to be there. They knew how hard she'd worked for the suffrage cause. "Mrs. Barnett, you must march!" they cried.

Ida was silent for a moment. She wished she'd stayed in the Windy City. She wished Alfreda's small hand still held hers.

Then her chin went up. Her famous dark eyes flashed.

"Why, ladies," she said. "Nothing could stop me."

And with five thousand women, Ida marched in the parade.

CHAPTER 9

Reporting on the Riots

Ida had quit the Afro-American Council in 1902. By that time, the council had been taken over by Booker T. Washington. It was no longer any good as a protest group.

But in 1909, Ida was one of the founding members of a new group. This group, unlike Mr. Washington, was clearly against the Jim Crow system. Its goal was equal rights for people of all races. Black people and white people joined to found the group. They called it the National Association for the Advancement of Colored People, or NAACP. Today the NAACP is the largest, strongest civil rights group in the nation.

It was a race riot that led to the founding of the NAACP. The people who began the group were alarmed by the riot. This was partly because it happened outside the South. Before long, there were more riots—often outside the South.

The greatest number of riots happened during and after the World War of 1914-1918. By that time, there were no young children in the Barnett household. The oldest boys had graduated from college. Even Ida, Jr., and Alfreda were in high school. Ida traveled much more often now.

It was a good thing Ida was traveling again. It meant she could go to places where the riots happened. Her firsthand reports on the riots provided badly needed truths. Without these truths, the fate of black Americans would have been even worse.

On July 2 and 3, 1917, a riot swept through East St. Louis, Illinois. The first news report said that many black people had died. Others had fled the city. Not much more was reported.

Two days after the first report, Ida was seated on a train. She wore a white linen dress and a hat of summer straw. She looked cool and calm. The conductor bent over to speak to her. "Your ticket says East St. Louis. It's very dangerous there right now. We'll take you on to St. Louis, across the river."

"I'll get off at East St. Louis," Ida said.

The conductor's eyebrows went up. "Haven't you read the papers? It's not safe for a colored person in East St. Louis!"

Ida pulled on her gloves. "We'll be in East St. Louis in five minutes," she said. "That's where I'm getting off." The conductor shrugged and went on down the aisle.

Ida stepped off the train into a nearly empty station. Young white men in khaki, wearing guns, were on patrol. They were members of the state militia, the National Guard.

The streets were busier than the station. Ida saw a

Red Cross truck parked at the corner. There were black women inside the truck. Not another black person was in sight—anywhere.

Ida went over to speak with the women. They said the truck had just brought them across the river from St. Louis. They were staying at a refugee camp in St. Louis. Most of the black people who had fled the riot were at the camp.

The Red Cross truck was taking the women to the places where they had lived—not to stay, but to see what was left.

"May I go along?" Ida asked the truck driver.

"If you want to," the driver said, "at your own risk."

All that day, Ida toured in the truck with the women. Many of the homes she saw had been looted. Some had been burned. Furniture had been smashed. The women took away what they could of their belongings—bedding, pots and pans. Some of them were crying. They were afraid to return to East St. Louis to live. They didn't know where they would go.

At the refugee camp, Ida interviewed more people. She was the first person to investigate the riot. She talked with both black people and white people at the camp. She had a lot of information by the time she returned to Chicago.

A day later, with some members of her church, Ida went to see the Illinois governor. She told him that at least fifty black people had been murdered in East St. Louis. Many more were wounded.

"They were attacked by white mobs," Ida said. "And do you know why? Because men of my race have jobs now in the factories. Evidently it's a crime for a black man to have a job! The state militia stood and watched as these innocent people were killed. They did nothing to protect them. Nothing."

"If that's true," the governor said, "it is an outrage."

"Why, sir, it's quite true!"

The governor promised to start an investigation. "Of course, we'll need people who witnessed these events," he added.

So Ida went back to East St. Louis, to line up witnesses. Meanwhile, however, black people were accused of riot and murder. At the trials that followed, ten black men were sentenced to long prison terms. Another was given life imprisonment. The white people who had started the riot received light sentences.

Ida did not give up. She wrote many articles telling the truth about the riots. She demanded justice for the black prisoners. Her stories were printed in an important black paper, the *Chicago Defender.* Helped by this publicity about their cases, all the men at last were freed. But it took many years.

During those years, there were more and more riots. One of the worst was in Ida's own city. For four days, in May of 1919, the streets of Chicago were like battle zones.

There was no trouble in the Barnetts' neighborhood. Ida was safe there. But she didn't stay there.

She went into the battle zones. Day and night, she went out to get the facts.

It wasn't always easy for Ida to keep going. Sometimes, on the strife torn streets, she felt fear. Yet she kept going because "somebody's got to stand up for our rights." She never felt sure anybody would "stand up," unless she stood up first.

Very soon after the Chicago riot, Ida heard about trouble elsewhere. This time it was in Arkansas. Trouble in the South was nothing new. But new things were happening in the South.

Black Southerners were beginning to fight back. They were starting to organize. By 1918, the NAACP had more members in the South than in the North. The white South could no longer depend on black people to *stay down.*

Black Southerners paid dearly for their new spirit. The white South tried even harder than in the past to frighten them. There were more lynchings. There was worse brutality.

The cruelty was unbelievable. In Georgia, in 1918, a white mob lynched a pregnant black woman. She was hanged to a tree. The mob poured gasoline on her and set her afire. A white man opened her belly with a knife. When the newborn baby fell out, the mob stomped out its life.

The horror of such acts *did* keep some black Southerners down. Yet others went on organizing. Among them was a group of cotton farmers in Arkansas. They formed a union. At market time, all refused to sell their cotton below market price.

The white cotton buyers did not want to pay black farmers a fair price. To teach black people a lesson, they staged a riot. Scores of black people were murdered. Others were jailed. The black farmers were accused of planning to murder white people and take their land. Their jailers beat and tortured them to confess to these lies. But they did not confess.

At the trial that followed, twelve black men were found guilty of murder. A white jury took just six minutes to decide their case. They were sentenced to die in the electric chair. Sixty-seven other black people were given long prison sentences.

In Chicago, Ida wrote a letter about the black farmers to the *Defender.* Reading it, people sent money to the paper for the legal defense of the men. Next, a protest meeting was held. Ida spoke there to a crowd of more than one thousand people. They agreed to send a protest wire to the governor of Arkansas. They also sent wires to the President and to members of Congress.

The governor knew that the whole country was watching Arkansas now. He put off the death date of the twelve men. He agreed to see to it that they got a new trial.

Now Ida had to travel again. She needed to interview the prisoners, to get their whole story. She was not sure she would succeed. A man from the NAACP had already tried it. The jailers tipped off some white thugs, who ran him out of town.

Ida had been run out of a Southern town herself. That was thirty years before. She had not been back to the South since.

Once more, Ida waved goodbye to Ferdinand from a train. In her purse was a letter that had been sent to the *Defender* by the men in jail. They had written to thank those who were trying to help them. They gave an address in Little Rock, Arkansas. It was the address of the mother of one of the men.

Early in the morning, Ida got off the train in Little Rock. The air of the South—that forgotten air—it smelled so sweet! Tears came to Ida's eyes. She remembered the past . . . . But a lot of the past was not so sweet, thought Ida. She wiped her eyes and hurried to the address she was carrying.

The wives and mothers of the men were waiting for Ida. They were going to visit the jailed men. Ida went with them. The jailers thought she was just another black wife or mother. Through the bars, Ida spoke quietly with the men. They gave her all the information she had come for.

Then the farmers sang and prayed. They asked God to forgive their enemies. They prayed to be received in heaven, since they were innocent.

Ida listened until the prayers and songs had ended. Then she moved to the bars. No guard was near to hear her words.

"Quit that talk about dying!" she said softly. "You believe that God is powerful? Then believe God is powerful enough to open these prison doors! Pray to be *freed.* Pray to *live!*"

Then Ida left. When she got home, she wrote a long article. Her story gave important new facts about the riot. Many people read it. Many more joined the fight to free the Arkansas men.

The following year, the twelve men were freed. The U.S. Supreme Court ruled, in 1923, that they hadn't had a fair trial. In time, all the other prisoners were freed, too.

About a year after the Supreme Court ruling, a young man knocked at the Barnetts' door. "Do you know me?" he asked Ida.

Ida replied, "I can't say that I do."

"I am one of the twelve men you came to see in Arkansas," said the young man. "I have come to thank you."

Ida brought Ferdinand and their daughters to meet the young man. He told them, "In the prison, Mrs. Barnett told us to stop talking about dying. She said if we had faith in God, we should pray to be freed. After that, we never talked about dying any more. We prayed for freedom. And now—all of us *are* free!"

Like the twelve men, Ida had faith. But Ida never believed that God works alone. She believed that women and men also had to work. For freedom. For justice.

Beginning with Ida B. Wells.

CHAPTER 10

Fighting to the End

The grocery shop bell tinkled. The March wind blew through the open door. Two women entered. One was young, the other middle aged. Both were well dressed.

Wearing a green apron, the black shop owner came forward. "Help you, ladies?" he said.

"Well, I hope so," the older woman said. "May we put this sign in your window?"

She held out the sign. It read: "Elect Ida B. Wells State Senator." The shop owner's face broke into a smile. "You sure can!" he said. "Now, wait. I'll just move these oranges— Hand me your sign. There!" He placed the sign in the window.

Both women smiled. "Thank you, sir!" said the older.

"Oh, you don't need to thank *me*. It's *her* we should thank. About time we got somebody honest running for office! Somebody who *cares* about people. Just look out there."

The shop owner nodded at the street. "One begging on one corner. One selling pencils on the other. Hungry! I give them day-old bread, maybe an apple. I can't feed all of them. Hard enough to feed my own self, times so bad. Think those colored politicians we elected *do* anything about it? They just want to line their own pockets. Mrs. Barnett, now—she *does* things!"

For the first time since entering, the younger woman spoke. "Oh, I know she does! Mrs. Barnett is my *hero!*"

"Good for you!" the shop owner said. "You know that center she and Lawyer Barnett set up? That was a mighty good thing. But now it's gone. Too many folks didn't *care.* I used to help out sometime. Gave a few dollar . . . . Wait a minute!"

The shop owner opened the cash register. He drew out a dollar bill. "Here." He handed the bill to the older woman. "Here's for Mrs. Barnett's campaign. You tell her Oscar, at Smith's Grocery, sent this here. I'd do better if I could."

The women thanked him. The shop bell tinkled as they left.

"Yes," Oscar Smith thought. "Mrs. Barnett—she *does* things!"

About a month later, Mr. Smith removed the sign from his window. The 1930 Republican primary election was over. Ida hadn't won. In fact, she had been badly beaten.

Ida had run as an independent. She had not been supported by either of the two wings of the Republican Party, called the "regulars" and the "liberals." Her support came only from a few groups, mostly women's groups.

Ida had not expected to win. She had used the campaign to talk about the needs of the poor. The Great Depression was causing a lot of suffering. Ida wanted to point out that politicians were not *doing* anything.

Though Ida hadn't expected to win, she'd hoped for more votes. She would have liked to know that more people agreed with her. She would have liked the party politicians to know it, too.

Ida had lost another election not many years before. That one was for president of the National Association of Colored Women, or NACW. This was the strong group Ida helped to form in the 1890s. (It is still a very strong group today.) It was to the NACW's first meeting that Ida had taken the infant Charles.

Ida felt more hurt about the NACW election than about losing the primary. She did not know the people who voted in the primary. But she *did* know the women in the NACW. It was important to her to feel that they trusted her.

And most of the women did trust Ida. But that wasn't the same thing as liking her! Ida's hot temper had flared at many of these women. Many had felt the lash of her sharp tongue.

To some, then, Ida was "my hero." To others she was "that bossy Ida Wells." In her sixties, Ida had a full, commanding figure. Her rich hair, turning silver, gleamed like a helmet. She was impressive—and when she frowned, some women were terror-stricken.

Ida clashed with men, too, in the groups she belonged to. She had helped to start the NAACP. But she angered some of its other leaders—men, women, black, white. Some thought she was too radical. She pushed for strong stands. She was scornful when the NAACP didn't move fast enough.

The NAACP had made a big push against lynching, starting in 1916. By 1918, it succeeded in getting President Wilson to make a public statement against lynching. Three years later, with NAACP pressure, a federal bill against lynching almost passed. The NAACP also did a lot of legal work in its anti-lynching fight.

The number of lynchings went down sharply. No one can say exactly why. But, for one thing, the South's leaders didn't like having such a lot of bad publicity for the region. For another, lynchers could no longer be so sure the law would protect them. Clearly, the NAACP's work had a lot to do with that.

But all this happened twenty-five years after Ida had begun her anti-lynching crusade. She had begun it all alone, in great danger. And nearly alone, she went on fighting, year after year.

Ida continued to fight, both alone and in groups. She fought every evil that came to her attention. At nearly seventy, she was still "standing up" and speaking out. Her pen scarcely ever stopped moving.

The words that flowed from her pen helped to change the history of Ida's time. They would go on having an effect on the history that followed her. But one day, Ida's pen stopped moving. She became ill suddenly and died four days later, in March 1931.

Ida's name and memory were kept alive by African-American women. In 1940, a Chicago housing project was named for her. It was the Ida B. Wells Club that worked to have Ida honored in this way. The project—called the Ida B. Wells Garden Homes houses seven thousand low-income people. It was low-income people Ida fought hardest to serve while she lived.

Before Ida died, she had written down most of the story of her life. Ida's daughter Alfreda knew that no writer could tell Ida's story better than Ida. Alfreda did the work of editing Ida's unfinished story. The book, titled *Crusade for Justice*, was published in 1970.

By then, the modern civil rights movement had brought many changes. White Americans had begun to look at black Americans with new respect. In Chicago, as in many other U.S. cities, a street was named for Dr. Martin Luther King, Jr. This is the street where the Barnett family had lived. To honor Ida, the government named the Ida B. Wells-Barnett House a National Monument.

It is no longer black women alone who keep Ida's memory alive. Today, white people as well as African-Americans are beginning to study her life, her stirring words. More and more people have learned about her. There are Ida B. Wells buttons, bookmarks, and posters.

One especially beautiful poster shows Ida as a young woman. The face is serious. The large eyes do not flash. They are thoughtful, dreaming. They seem to be gazing at the future. Her words appear below the picture.

Our work, Ida says, *has only begun. Our race must strike the blow if they would be free.*

About the Author

SUE DAVIDSON is a writer and editor who co-authored *You Can Be Free: An Easy-to-Read Handbook for Abused Women* (Seal, 1989). She is the co-editor of *A Needle, A Bobbin, A Strike: Women Needleworkers in America* (Temple University Press, 1984) and of *The Maimie Papers* (The Feminist Press, 1977). Her writing has appeared in national publications including *The Progressive, The Nation, Commonweal, New Directions for Women, Frontiers: A Journal of Women Studies*, and the *Nonviolent Activist*.

Davidson is a longtime participant in movements for peace and social justice. Originally from Texas, where she worked on the editorial staff of the *Galveston Daily News*, she makes her home in Seattle.

Selected Titles from Seal Press

You Can Be Free: *An Easy-to-Read Handbook for Abused Women* by Ginny NiCarthy and Sue Davidson. $6.95, 0-931188-68-7 A simplified version of the bestselling *Getting Free,* the most important self-help resource book of the domestic violence movement.

The Black Women's Health Book: *Speaking for Ourselves* edited by Evelyn C. White. $14.95, 0-931188-86-5 This pioneering anthology addresses the health issues facing today's black woman. Contributors include Fay Wattleton, Byllye Avery, Alice Walker, Audre Lorde, Angela Y. Davis and dozens more.

Nervous Conditions by Tsitsi Dangarembga. $9.95, 0-931188-74-1 A lyrical story of a Zimbabwean girl's coming-of-age and a compelling narrative of the devastating human loss involved in the colonization of one culture by another.

I Change Worlds by Anna Louise Strong. $7.95, 0-931188-05-9 This fascinating autobiography, available for the first time since 1935, covers Strong's career as a journalist at the turn of the century, including her travels in Russia, Poland, Spain and China.

No More Secrets by Nina Weinstein. $8.95, 1-878067-00-1 Mandy, a strong and funny and sometimes lonely teenager, struggles with memories of sexual abuse and begins the process of healing.

Seal Press, founded in 1976 to provide a forum for women writers and feminist issues, has many other books of fiction, non-fiction and poetry. You may order directly from us at 3131 Western Avenue, Suite 410, Seattle, WA 98121 (add 15% of total book order for shipping and handling). Write to us for a free catalog or if you would like to be on our mailing list.